A Treasure Chest of Teachin

I Teach Kindergarten!

Peggy Campbell-Rush

Crystal Springs BOOKS

Peterborough, New Hampshire
1-800-321-0401 • www.crystalsprings.com

© 2000 Crystal Springs Books

Printed in the United States of America

Published by Crystal Springs Books
75 Jaffrey Road
PO Box 500
Peterborough, NH 03458
1-800-321-0401
www.sde.com, www.crystalsprings.com

Library of Congress Cataloging-in-Publication Data (U.S.)

Campbell-Rush, Peggy.
   I teach kindergarten! : a treasure chest of teaching wisdom / Peggy
Campbell-Rush. —1st ed.
[160] p. : ill. ; cm. (I Teach)
Includes bibliographical references and index.
Summary: All aspects of teaching, development, and activities relating
to kindergartners are included.
ISBN 1-884548-34-2
1. Kindergarten. 2. Early childhood education. I. Title. 2. Series.
372.218 21   LB1169.C33 2000

Vice President, Merchandise and Publishing: Lorraine Walker
Editor and Publishing Projects Coordinator: Cathy Kingery

Illustrations: Phyllis Pittet
Cover, book design, and production: Soosen Dunholter
Back cover photograph: Lou Sapienza

Dedication

To Jimbo, Mackensie, Morgan, Taylor, Muzzy, Big Bob, Honey, and Chots—my rocks, my angels, and my circle of love.

Table of Contents

® =This chapter contains reproducibles, samples, and/or sample student work.

® =This chapter contains reproducibles, samples, and/or sample student work.

® =This chapter contains reproducibles, samples, and/or sample student work.

Foreword

This has to be the best handbook yet for busy kindergarten teachers. The practical advice is readily accessible and right on target. It is to the classroom what a navigation chart is to a voyage.

But Peggy Campbell-Rush is no armchair chart-maker. She writes from long experience. More than that—she writes from long and successful experience. She knows how to make children into winners, parents into friends, and the classroom into a place of fun and efficient learning, and she shares her secrets in clear, simple language. Step-by-step procedures, nonfail strategies, affirmation, enthusiasm, and lively creativity all come together in this book to make education a wholly rewarding process for both teacher and student.

I have seen Peggy Campbell-Rush at work, and I am aware of the impact she has on her young students and on her fellow teachers. She is also valuable to other authors. From time to time she has tested my manuscripts in her classroom for me, and I have always been impressed by her perception and wisdom.

Well done, Peggy! You have created a winner to make winners!

Joy Cowley

Acknowledgments

My sincere thanks and deepest gratitude go to:

Cathy Kingery, Meredith Reed O'Donnell, and Susan Dunholter, who turned jumbled computer disks and mountains of paper into a grand manuscript.

Irv Richardson, whose phone call at the eleventh hour saved me from caving in to my doubts and fears.

Joy Cowley, a joy and inspiration to all teachers everywhere.

Lou Sapienza, my personal friend and professional photographer.

Beth Bayuk and the TAWL group, for their visionary push years ago to take our school to a higher level, and for taking me into their fold and mentoring me into the teacher I have become.

Linda N., Ann S., Christine D., and Denise N., first for being my gifted professional colleagues, and second for being my close personal friends who brought me back   from the depths of cancer.

Jenn W.—You GO, girl!

My husband, Jim, who is now and always has been the wind beneath my wings.

My children, Mac, Mo, and Tay, my three resilient miracles who show me each day that life has magic woven into the fibers of the moment.

My parents, who were always there with a loving hand to either push me forward or slow me down—but were always lifting me up.

Chots and Honey, who are real, live, earth angels.

And, finally, to Jim Grant, who believed in my knowledge and experience enough to ask one simple question: "Peggy, why don't you write a book?"

Widely Held Expectations for Kindergartners

Developmental Expectations

Whether you are new to teaching kindergarten or have been at it for years, you know that five- and six-year-olds are at a very distinct level of development. The kindergarten year is as important in a person's academic career as his/her freshman year in college. These two occasions are certainly equally emotional for most parents!

We hear and read a lot about developmentally appropriate practices in kindergarten. The phrase "developmentally appropriate" can mean a lot of different things to different people. For instance, in a position statement adopted by its governing board in 1996, the National Association for the Education of Young Children (NAEYC) defined a developmentally appropriate practice as "the outcome of a process of teacher decision-making that draws on at least three critical, interrelated bodies of knowledge: (1) what teachers know about how children develop and learn; (2) what teachers know about the individual children in their group; and (3) knowledge of the social and cultural context in which those children live and learn."

To me, "developmentally appropriate" means that we, as teachers, recognize that five- and six-year-olds are unique in their social, emotional, cognitive, and physical abilities. It also means that everything we do in our kindergarten class is appropriate for each child's stage of development.

Research by Eric Jensen (1998) suggests that we should consider a three-year span of abilities within a kindergarten classroom to be normal. As teachers, we must meet all our students' individual and collective needs on a developmentally appropriate level. This means saying NO to the idea of a push-down curriculum from first grade. It also means that, if we move from a half-day to a full-day program, we don't add more curriculum to fill up the time. And it means that we provide time for children to love school and teach them the skills necessary to become readers, writers, and mathematicians (among other things) in the future.

Finally, it means we don't promise to make every child a reader by the end of the kindergarten year. We are there to provide the groundwork of skills necessary for each child to *become* a reader and learner of many other things in first grade.

Question & Answer

Does one style of teaching work best?

Having taught for over twenty years, I can emphatically say NO! You must pull the best ideas from every teaching method, great mentor, idea book, research, theory, and experience you have ever had, heard, or read about. If the method you are using does not match a particular child, then do what works for that child. All children do not learn the same way, so our teaching must address diversities.

I am reminded of the phrase "spray and pray" when I think of the practice of adopting only one teaching method and hoping you have addressed all your students' needs and learning styles. Trust me—you haven't.

Reach out. Visit other classrooms and see other teachers teach, attend teaching seminars specifically geared toward kindergarten, read professional magazines, go on-line, read books on methodology, and try different teaching approaches to see what works best to make every child a learner achieving his/her maximum potential.

We cannot—and should not—be forced to engage in practices, such as trying to get all kindergartners to read, that are developmentally inappropriate for the kindergarten-age child. Teachers—not necessarily administrators—know their students the best. We accept each child at his/her current level and work to move them all to a higher plain.

It seems more and more that kindergarten is the last place where children have an opportunity to play in school. Make sure you *keep playtime*. Don't let anyone tell you to throw it out of your daily schedule. Play is developmentally appropriate. This is where children have a chance to do all the following things:

- stretch their imaginations
- interact with peers
- clean up after themselves
- be physically active
- have fun
- develop story lines
- make architectural structures
- create masterpieces
- express feelings
- form identities
- form collaborative groups
- sustain interests
- get messy
- form social skills
- monitor their own activities
- bond with friends
- develop small- and large-motor coordination
- engage in fantasy
- direct plays
- share
- let off steam
- show their real selves
- practice life skills in a safe place
- work toward a goal
- just PLAY!

The above is not a definitive list, so don't hesitate to add some items of your own. Then if anyone ever tries to make your kindergarten purely academic, show that person your list!

Another important concept to keep in mind is that we need to view the kindergarten curriculum as a pie divided into four equal parts: social, emotional, cognitive, and physical. It is crucial to give each part of this pie equal attention and importance. If any one of these parts gets more attention than the others, our students will grow unevenly and miss opportunities to grow into well-rounded persons.

This will become evident not only in the classroom in later years as these children grow up, but also throughout their lives. If academics is the main thrust, then the children miss out on social interaction and emotional growth, which are of paramount importance when they grow up and enter the workforce. But if social growth is the main objective, then the children miss opportunities to learn needed academic and physical skills that will be used in later grades. So, you can see that each area needs to be balanced and integrated with the others.

In the next four sections, I'll discuss these areas in depth and outline the widely held expectations in each for kindergarten children.

Social

By the time they enter kindergarten, it is very helpful for children to have spent some time with children of their own age. Five- and six-year-olds are generally ready to give up being totally egocentric and self-centered. They can stretch their emotions to include others more and more as the kindergarten year progresses. For example, they start to empathize with a friend who is hurt or sad, their play becomes more group-oriented, and they begin to notice the activities of the world around them.

This is the time for these children to take a giant step away from their parents and enter a world where they are one of many rather than one of a few. But this is a hard lesson to learn for children who have had little social exposure prior to kindergarten.

Kindergarten children are naturally a curious, friendly, open, and honest group. They can be expected to do the following:

- interact with their peers
- speak to peers and teachers in full sentences
- learn classmates' names
- choose a partner to work with
- sit in a group and take turns
- wait for a short period of time
- initiate interactions with familiar adults
- engage in social problem-solving
- express choices
- sustain play for five to ten minutes
- develop empathy for others
- follow the rules and routines of the class
- show their unique personalities

These are not hard-and-fast rules to be checked off one by one. Instead, they are a general overview of the kindergarten child. We certainly don't want to make cookie-cutter kids who all conform to a rigid standard, but general expectations make for a better environment for learning and growing. We want children to be who they are, and we need to find and celebrate their uniqueness in our classrooms. If you find that a child lacks a good number of these social skills, you may want to focus your attention on his/her deficiencies in this area.

We can encourage maximum social growth by making our classroom inviting and safe. By "safe," I mean a place where all children are valued, recognized, celebrated, and nurtured.

This brings us to the emotional-growth area.

Emotional

Brain research tells us the brain's first priority is survival. In a very basic and subconscious way, we evaluate new situations to determine whether they are safe. If we perceive a threat, the brain employs the "fight or flight" response and decides on an instant reaction.

If our classrooms do not provide a safe, nurturing environment, we may be forcing our students' brains to perceive a threat and go into survival mode. When that happens, all higher-order thinking, reasoning skills, social interactions, and academic responses are then shut down, or at least severely hampered.

Keep in mind that the word *threat* does not always mean physical harm. Threats can include verbal put-downs, different learning styles, an inability to speak the language, or a curriculum that drives students too far, too fast.

Emotional well-being forms early in a child's life and is fostered at home by a nurturing family and a stimulating environment. We know that many children lack that foundation and come into our classrooms fearful and undernourished emotionally. Some are victims of emotional abuse, which is nearly impossible to see tangible signs of.

Children of kindergarten age should be able to do the following:

- separate easily from their parents within a week or so
- form a friendship with one or more children in the room
- converse with you at their comfort level
- have a positive self-concept
- transition from task to task and from one adult to another
- accept being corrected
- discern between right and wrong
- be happy at school

In addition, they should be able to feel welcome, safe, encouraged, loved, and nurtured while they are in your classroom. This emotional balance fosters optimum learning.

Question & Answer

What should I do for a child who is over and above the kindergarten expectations?

REMEMBER that even a gifted child is still maturationally a kindergartner. Don't rush to add more academics to this child's curriculum just because you think he or she can do it. This child will be pushed enough in life, so make sure he/she gets sufficient time to socialize and play.

ENRICH this student with picture books that are on a higher-than-normal reading or comprehension level.

LOOK for ways to give this child some extra opportunities to explore topics of interest in depth.

PROVIDE mentors who can help this child investigate areas of interest beyond the kindergarten curriculum.

DON'T pressure the child to be entirely academic-oriented. Know that he/she is multidimensional; pay attention to his/her social, emotional, physical, and maturational development.

DON'T use this student as a second teacher, helping other children in the class. This will single out this child as different.

OFTEN a gifted child is lacking in some areas. For example, I have had children in my class who were able to read on a fifth-grade level, multiply, and divide, but unable to cut out a simple square with a pair of scissors. Make sure that you, and everyone else who teaches this child, recognizes the child's need to be well rounded and balanced.

READ! Provide this child with lots of reading material. Books can be great teachers. Also, give this child plenty of access to a computer so he/she can use it as an information resource.

GET HELP. See if there is another teacher who can spend some time with this child and do some one-on-one enrichment.

RECOGNIZE and celebrate the unique and special talents this child possesses!

Cognitive

Some children will enter your classroom barely knowing their first and last name, while others will be reading chapter books! The diverse nature of kindergarten children's prior experiences is so broad that I am still amazed at what I observe after twenty years of teaching.

As I mentioned earlier, there is no cookie-cutter mold we can use to ensure that all kindergartners will know certain things. They know what they know, and that's it. We are faced with the task of taking them from where they are cognitively and moving them along as far as they can go during the year they spend with us. You will be able to make more progress with some children than with others, but each child will grow and blossom under your watchful eye.

The students in your class will have a tremendous range of skills, and you may be expected to ensure they leave kindergarten all on the same level. This will not happen. You will not be able to make a child attain two years' worth of progress and growth in one year. Don't allow anyone—not parents, not administrators—to pressure you to push any child beyond what he/she is maturationally ready to handle. All children grow at their own rate, and a child will only suffer in the end if you push, push, push.

Ideally, on a cognitive level, kindergarten children:

- know their first and last name
- have their gender identity established
- have been read to
- have had prior experiences that fostered thought and conversation

Question & Answer

What should I do about the parent who wants his/her child to learn more content than you feel is appropriate in kindergarten?

I run into this problem quite often. You need to learn a lot about the parent before you address this issue. First find out WHY the parent wants this to happen. Sometimes the child is an above-average student, in which case I agree to provide him/her with more learning opportunities. But very often, the parent has issues he/she does not communicate to me. Some of these include a need to "keep up with the Joneses," or the parent is very socially tuned in and wants to tout that "my child is learning all the continents and oceans in kindergarten!," or this is his/her first or only child and he/she does not remember that being in kindergarten is not all about academics.

I keep reminding this parent that, as mentioned earlier, a child's development is like a pie cut into four pieces: social, emotional, cognitive, and physical. If any one of those pieces is given more emphasis than the others in kindergarten, the child will grow unevenly.

Be sure you conference often with this type of parent. Sometimes you need to educate the parents as much as you educate your students.

Often a parent who wants his/her child to learn more judges your program by the papers the child brings home. But if you have a hands-on curriculum like mine, the children bring home no papers! Instead, I take photos of all the activities we do to ensure that the parents can see and support my hands-on program. I paste the photos onto construction paper and add captions explaining what's happening in each one. I then laminate the sheets of paper; bind them into a book, putting a parent comment page in the back; and route the book home to each child's house once a month.

I can't tell you how many parents have made comments like "I can't believe you get so much done in a day!" or "The day is packed full with so much activity and information!" or "This is so much more than what my older child did in kindergarten!" A picture is worth a thousand words!

Finally, remind these parents that kindergarten children are only five and six years old. Although their minds may be advanced, they still need to be with their peer group and grow socially, emotionally, and physically.

If a child enters your classroom with very few prior experiences in life, has never been read to, and is intellectually immature, you have a big job cut out for you. You need to assess right away what skills this child has so that you can begin to teach him/her the skills necessary to thrive during the kindergarten year. (See Chapter 3, "Assessment," for specific ideas.)

For the child who shows up in your classroom ready for kindergarten, your regular curriculum and activities will provide the growth opportunities he/she needs to have a productive year. As mentioned in the previous Q&A, you can provide enrichment activities for the gifted child.

Physical

Children in kindergarten are naturally a physical bunch. They love to run, jump, climb, and explore their world from a tactile point of view. Generally, kindergarten-age children can do the following:

- run
- jump
- climb steps
- hop
- draw
- color
- copy a shape
- dress themselves (not counting tying shoes)
- drink from a cup
- sit and listen to a story
- draw a person
- attend to bathroom needs independently
- cut on a straight line
- build a tower of seven to ten blocks
- build with simple construction toys
- know whether they are right- or left-handed

One of the major dilemmas for a kindergarten teacher is the child who cannot hold a pencil, crayon, and/or pair of scissors. Either the child has not had any prior exposure to these items or has developed his/her own style of improper grip and was never corrected. Improper grips are hard to correct, but you must try to redirect this child to use a grip that is more appropriate for writing, coloring, and cutting.

The activities listed on the next page will exercise the entire arm, strengthen the wrist, and make the hand muscles work.

Question & Answer

What can I do to help a child who has an improper pencil grip?

Holding a pencil is an important skill in kindergarten. But many children come to school either without this skill or having developed improper ways of doing it. There are several things you can do to help these children.

Between the ages of four and six, children develop the mature tripod grip necessary for holding a pencil correctly and using it to write. Adults have a pocket, called the Palmer Arch, in their palm. (To see it, hold your hand flat out in front of you; you'll notice the rounded indentation in your palm.) In contrast, children's palms are flat, which indicates that the muscles in this region are still immature.

You can do many strengthening activities to facilitate hand and finger strength. First, don't assume that a child *must* use a pencil to develop the muscles in the hand. There are many other ways to increase hand strength. The first is to do lots of vertical activities, such as the following:

- working on a vertical chalkboard or dry-erase board

- using a felt board or magnet board mounted on the wall

- working with puzzles, patterns, Play-Doh, or pegboard activities on a slanted surface (There's no need to buy an expensive slant-board for this. Just open a three-ring binder and lay it flat, front side down, on a flat table or work surface.)

- finger-painting with water on a vertical chalkboard

- drawing on chart paper mounted to a wall or easel

You should note a child's body position while he/she is working. There's a lot to be said for sitting up straight, having your chair pushed in, and holding your head erect. These are not just phrases your mother used to use; correct body alignment enables all the muscles to work in unison and support one another. Strength and stability in the large muscles, such as those in the shoulders, head, and back, aid in hand and wrist development.

You need not begin with pencil/paper activities right off the bat at the start of the kindergarten year. You can get the same muscle-strengthening results from some of these activities:

- using large needles to sew through loose fabric, such as burlap
- using a nutcracker to crack small twigs (over a large tray!)
- picking up small objects, such as beans or coins
- picking up small objects with one hand and hiding them in the palm without help from the other hand
- putting together construction toys, such as LEGOs or K'NEX
- playing dice games, jacks, or marbles
- using flip cards
- ripping paper (Children in my class love to get into a big open box, rip paper to their heart's content, and throw it on the floor of the box. It's lots of fun and requires no cleanup.)
- stirring sand or water

- gardening
- making paper airplanes
- using sidewalk chalk on pavement
- using a hole puncher
- using a stapler
- putting magnets on a magnetic board and pulling them off again
- rolling a pea-size piece of Play-Doh around and around between the first finger and thumb, second finger and thumb, and so on
- doing finger gymnastics by tapping one finger at a time on the table or tapping it together with the thumb (Do this with one hand and then the other.)

One great idea is to make a tennis-ball puppet: Simply take a tennis ball and make a two-inch slit in it. Use your fingers to grasp the ball on either side of the slit and squeeze. This should make the ball open at the slit. You can manipulate it to look like a mouth opening and closing. I have seen children in my class pick up a bean with one hand and "feed" it into the mouth of the tennis ball. You can decorate the ball with a face or make it look like an animal. (A fish looks great!)

When you are ready to introduce pencils and the tripod grip to a child, let him/her choose which size, style, and shape of pencil he/she feels most comfortable using. Show the child how the thumb and index and middle fingers grab the pencil in a tripod grasp. Tell the child that his/her fingers should move with the pencil as he/she writes.

If necessary, let the child use a pencil grip. If you don't have any, ball up a piece of paper towel and place it in the palm of the child's hand to facilitate the finger curl of the tripod grip.

Some children might need to use a four-finger grip to start with. Once they get more muscle control, they can move the ring finger off the pencil and use the three-finger tripod grip.

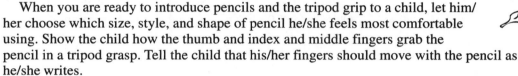

Question & Answer

What can I do for children who have poor muscle tone and can't grasp a pencil?

For these children, writing or working on a slanted surface helps a lot. In addition, working on a vertical surface stimulates stability in the entire arm, from the shoulder to the fingers. Do lots of small-muscle activities. Do not force a child to use a pencil for everything: Provide markers, crayons, or paints as alternatives. If poor muscle tone is a big problem, consult an occupational therapist for help with specific in-tervention activities.

Question & Answer

What should I do for the child who has not yet established hand dominance (right- or left-handedness)?

Bilateral integration refers to the two sides of the brain and body working together to do a task. By the time a child enters kindergarten, he/she should be able to cross over the midline of the body with either hand to retrieve or receive items on the opposite side of the body. Kindergarten children should be able to tell you whether they are right- or left-handed; if they can't, at least they can show you which hand they use.

Children without bilateral integration usually have not determined which hand is their strong or dom-inant hand. You can help these children by doing lots of crossover activities, such as the following:

- hopscotch
- Simon Says
- putting one arm behind the back and using the other to retrieve items
- throwing and catching
- crossing one hand across the chest and giving yourself a pat on the back
- touching body parts on one side of the body with the opposite hand

All these activities encourage the brain to make its two sides work together simultaneously. If you feel that a child has severe deficiencies in this area, it can be an indication of neurological problems. Trust your instincts and ask for outside help.

A child who still has not estab-lished hand dominance by the middle or end of kindergarten should also raise a red flag. This might be a sign of neurological imbalance; if you suspect this, get help from your school's child study team or outside professionals.

Is there an easy way to show children how to use scissors?

First make sure the scissors in your classroom are the right size for little hands. Then show the children how their fingers can "point the way." Use your hand to demonstrate how they should curl their fingers and extend the first finger into a pointing gesture. Have them put the thumb through the top hole, and the last three fingers through the bottom hole. The pointer finger will still be out, pointing the way to what they want to cut.

In sum, viewing a kindergarten child's development and needs as a four-piece, equally sliced pie will help you keep a balanced curriculum. Don't let anyone try to force you into giving more emphasis to one particular developmental area and thereby neglecting one or more of the others. Kindergarten is a year for optimum growth in all four areas.

Children need the time and opportunity to experiment with life and learn through play and fun. As teachers, we are masters of that art!

Academic Expectations

Reading, Listening, and Speaking

You and your colleagues should set your exit goals at the beginning of the school year. That way you can work backward from these established goals to plan activities, lessons, units of study, and themes. Your knowledge of the exit goals/skills will help you plan so that you facilitate the learning and academic growth of your students.

Use the following list of goals and related activities as a guide while you develop one that fits your specific classroom, curriculum, and state standards.

Book-Handling Skills:

- knowing the front and back of a book
- knowing how to turn the pages without skipping
- knowing where the print is

Idea: Have each child bring in the front panel of a favorite cereal box. Bind the panels together to make a book. The magic of this book is that even if a child holds it upside down, he/she will immediately recognize it, and the illustrations are bright, appealing, and well known to the children. And because the book is made out of cardboard, it will withstand a lot of handling!

Picture-Reading:

- Making up a story related to the picture clues on each page.
- Understanding the difference between a letter and a word.

Idea: Play the game "hangman" (although I play a variation called "draw a cat" to avoid the hangman connotation). I seat the children in a group in front of the board and draw lines to indicate the number of letters in the word I am thinking of.

The children then guess letters. If they are correct, I put the letter in the appropriate space. If they are incorrect, I write the letter on the side of the board and draw a part of a cat. I like to give the children lots of chances to beat me, so the cat has lots of parts.

Usually the children manage to fill in all the letters of the word before I finish drawing the cat. While playing this game, I keep a running tally of my score versus theirs, thus teaching them how to use tally marks and count by fives.

I also use this game to teach the difference between vowels and consonants. For this variation, I make the children guess only vowels until all the vowels in the word are filled in. Then we move on to guessing the consonants in the word.

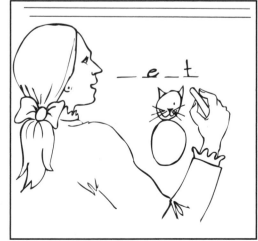

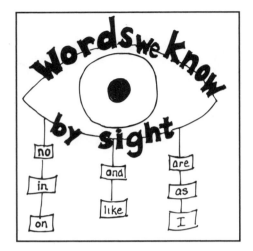

Recognize own name and other key words dictated by your curriculum

Idea: To keep the sight words that we are currently learning prominent in the classroom, I write them on three- by five-inch note cards and put them up on the alphabet word wall. I also keep another set handy so that if we are waiting in line to go somewhere, the children can look at them as I hold each one up. I also write them on a big eyeball labeled "Words We Know by Sight" that hangs from the center of the room.

Recognize the entire alphabet

Idea: Put alphabet strips everywhere! I even have two—one over the toilet and one on the wall opposite the toilet—in the kindergarten bathroom. It is so cute to hear someone singing the alphabet song in the bathroom!

I also use alphabet strips to send home after I conference with a child on recognition of alphabet letters. Each child helps me fill his/hers out. This gives the parent something tangible to work on with the child, and it indicates specific letters for the parent to help the child with. I keep a record of everything I send home.

Hear and produce rhyming words

Idea: I send home a "rhyming bag" with one child a day all year long. The child puts an item in the bag and thinks of a word that rhymes with the name of that item. During circle time each day, we all chant the following rhyme; the child supplies the clue for us to guess what is in the bag.

> I have something for you to see.
>
> It was picked by little old me.
>
> I am going to give you a clue
>
> So you can guess it, too.
>
> It rhymes with _____.

Produce the sounds of the alphabet letters . . . with the possible exception of the short vowel sounds and the letters *q, w, y,* and *x*

Idea: Play a variation of alphabet bingo. Instead of showing or saying a letter, give the sound of a letter. You can reinforce that sound by showing the letter on the bingo board.

Retell a story

Idea: Make "story boxes." This is an activity that parents can help you with. I first identify parents who are willing to help with projects by sending home a volunteer request letter (see Chapter 5, "Parents as Partners"). I then send these parents a favorite storybook and a large shoebox and ask them to fill the box with pictures, toys, and other props that will aid in the retelling of that story. I am amazed at the creativity of some parents! Some books that I have asked parents to help with include *The Three Little Pigs, The Mitten,* and *Henny Penny and the Napping House*. The children use these boxes to retell stories by themselves or with classmates.

Begin to track print

Idea: Make sure you have print (i.e., charts, poems, songs, alphabet charts, words, etc.) all over your room. I give my children time to "read the room" whenever they have a free moment after completing a project. I also keep lots of "tracking tools" in a large bucket for the children to use. These include fake fingers (from Halloween), gloves stuffed with cotton batting and mounted on dowels, flashlights, wands, back scratchers, and feather dusters. I even put out Bugles snack crackers every so often. The cone-shaped crackers fit perfectly on little fingers, and once the children are done tracking the print, they can eat the crackers! All these devices encourage children to track the print they see.

Show an interest in books

Idea: Researchers agree that for children to be interested in books, they need to have access to them. Often parents do not have books at home and do not go to the library. You should send books home every night with your students. Of course, that is easier said than done in schools where the budget is reduced or limited each year. Try putting a bulletin in your school newsletter asking for book donations (used or new), having parents scour yard sales for books, using the bonus points you or your friends receive from book clubs, making your own books (a good project for students in upper grades to do for the kindergarten children), and buying books whenever your school budget allows.

I use a book bag to get books into my students' homes. Inside the bag I enclose the letter found on the following page.

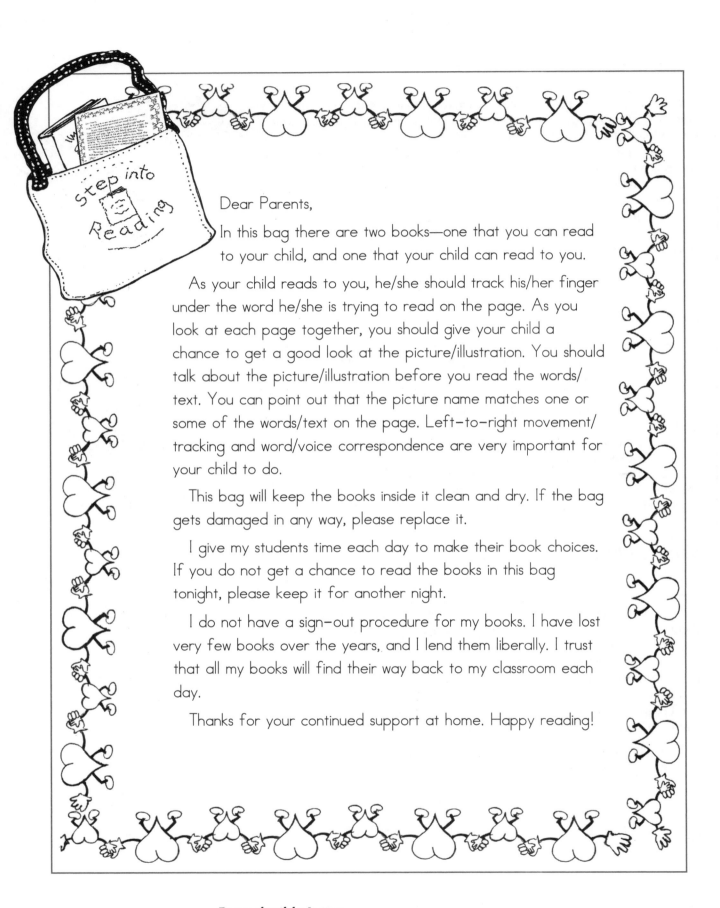

Dear Parents,

In this bag there are two books—one that you can read to your child, and one that your child can read to you.

As your child reads to you, he/she should track his/her finger under the word he/she is trying to read on the page. As you look at each page together, you should give your child a chance to get a good look at the picture/illustration. You should talk about the picture/illustration before you read the words/ text. You can point out that the picture name matches one or some of the words/text on the page. Left-to-right movement/ tracking and word/voice correspondence are very important for your child to do.

This bag will keep the books inside it clean and dry. If the bag gets damaged in any way, please replace it.

I give my students time each day to make their book choices. If you do not get a chance to read the books in this bag tonight, please keep it for another night.

I do not have a sign-out procedure for my books. I have lost very few books over the years, and I lend them liberally. I trust that all my books will find their way back to my classroom each day.

Thanks for your continued support at home. Happy reading!

Reproducible Letter

Oral Language

Retell the main parts of a story after being read to

Idea: Always buy two copies of a favorite book. Use one for reading to the children, and use the other for cutting out pictures. Lay out the pictures on the floor or tape them up on the board for story sequencing. You can also cut apart pictures of the main characters in a story to make puzzles.

When retelling, you are teaching students the following skills:

- speaking in complete sentences
- articulating a sentence to explain one's artwork
- interacting with classmates
- contributing ideas to discussions
- attempting to read own writing
- making predictions

Idea: Stop in the middle of a story occasionally and ask the children to predict what they think will happen next. Accept all responses. Before you read on, say, "Let's find out what the author has written." That way, you are not labeling any predictions as right or wrong.

Produce rhyming words

Idea: I love to sing the oldies song "The Name Game." The children love it when I rhyme their names as instructed in the song; for example, "Peggy, Peggy, Bo, Beggy; Banana, Fanna, Fo, Feggy; Fee, Fi, Mo, Meggy; Peggy." I find that they learn the song quickly, too.

Students should also be able to:

Participate in sharing time (e.g., show and tell, class meeting)

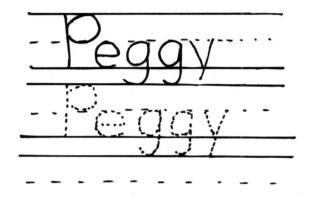

Writing

Write own name (first and last)

Idea: I provide practice papers where I write the child's name on the top line and dot it on the second line (see the example at left) so the child can trace the letters in a dot-to-dot fashion. Then I leave a blank line at the bottom of the paper for the child to practice writing his/her name on his/her own.

Write print-like symbols

Idea: Make time each week to do journal writing. Use paper that is blank on the top half for drawing a picture and lined on the bottom half for writing letters and words. Or you can use completely blank paper so the children can draw and write anywhere on the paper they choose.

Write some or all of the letters of the alphabet

Idea: The children have fun getting with partners and writing all the letters of the alphabet in order. I give each pair of partners a sentence strip (available in all school supply catalogs). One child starts by writing *A;* the other child writes *B;* the first child then writes *C;* and so on, with the children continuing to take turns until the alphabet is completed. I give those children who need it an alphabet strip to use as a resource.

Students should also be able to:

• produce a journal entry based on a picture drawing

• write from left to right

Read back own writing

Idea: After each journal-writing session, give the children some journal-share time. Each child can share with the class what he/she wrote in his/her journal.

- writing beginning letter sounds for words
- writing ending sounds for words
- writing medial sounds for words (This may be too advanced for some kindergarten students.)
- putting spaces between words

Idea: Teach the children about "spaghetti and meatball" letters and words: A strand of spaghetti goes between the letters in a word, and a meatball fits between the words in a sentence. You can also use the idea of a baseball and bat: The bat fits between the letters, and the ball goes between the words. I often supply my students with tongue depressors to use as spacing sticks while writing in their journals.

- beginning a sentence with a capital letter
- ending a sentence with a mark of punctuation

Idea: To highlight punctuation and writing tasks, I make writing rubrics, which I hang on the wall. On the bottom of eight brightly colored twelve-by eighteen-inch sheets of construction paper, I write one of the following sentences:

I can draw a picture.

I can write letters.

I can write words.

I can make a capital letter.

I can make a period.

I can make an exclamation point.

I can make a question mark.

I can write a sentence.

I photocopy one page from each of the children's journals and highlight each child's page on one of these sheets. As you can see, there is a category for the lowest achieving student (I can draw a picture.) as well as the highest (I can write a sentence.). I review these categories with the children before they begin writing in their journals, and I change the displayed papers about once a month.

Students should also be able to:

Know the difference between uppercase and lowercase letters

Phonological Awareness

Ability to:

- auditorially recognize, understand, and reproduce rhyming words
- clap hands or follow the rhythm of songs, chants, rhyming books, and poems
- hear sounds at the beginning, middle, and end of a word
- stretch out a word slowly and clap it back together (e.g., cccccaaaaattttt—**cat**)

Idea: Get a Slinky toy. In front of the children, slowly stretch the coils while you sound out a word. Then clap it back together as you say the word as a whole. This gives visual and tactile learners the benefit of seeing and feeling a word being segmented.

Describe an object

Idea: Take a lunch box and write the phrase "Mystery Box" on the lid. Send it home with one child per day. That child puts something inside. The next day, he/she gives the class clues about the identity of what is inside the box by using describing words. I usually spend about three weeks at the beginning of the school year putting things of mine in the box and bringing them in. This way, I model describing an object until I feel the children have caught on to the concept.

Students should also be able to:

- recognize when a group of words all begin with the same sound
- successfully master the sound/symbol correlation for at least three-quarters of the alphabet

Math

Count to thirty or beyond

Idea: I use every available opportunity to count out loud with the children—for example, at a transition time, or while we are waiting in line to go into the cafeteria or waiting for children to finish cleaning up.

Participate in graphing activities

Idea: Have the children take a two- by two-inch piece of paper, draw their face on it, and write their name under it. (I help them if the space is too small for them to be successful.) I then adhere a magnet strip on the back. We use these pictures throughout the year to create, on the magnetic board, graphs and surveys of things we like, don't like, etc.

Complete a simple pattern

Idea: Do lots of patterning as you line up each day. You can line up by boy/girl, by shoes/sneakers, or by long hair/short hair. (It was funny a few years ago when I was bald from chemotherapy and the children did not know where I would fit into the last pattern!)

Participate in measurement activities

Idea: Use standard tools (e.g., rulers, yardsticks, tape measures) and nonstandard tools (e.g., Unifix cubes, hands, feet, towers of blocks) when teaching measurement.

Identify basic shapes

Idea: Use shapes as name tags for the children if you label their seating assignments, or put shapes on their tables so you can call on certain tables (e.g., "Anyone who has a triangle on their table may line up now.").

Students should also be able to:

- identify position (e.g., top, middle, bottom, before, after, between, left, right)
- use attributes to classify objects
- sort items
- write numbers one to ten

Learn time and money concepts

Idea: Nothing teaches the concept of money better than spending it! If there is a store near your school, take a class trip there. At the beginning of our money unit, I ask each child to bring in from home a dollar's worth of change: two quarters, three dimes, three nickels, and five pennies. I put this money in individual film canisters (available for the asking at most photo shops) labeled with each child's name. After using this money throughout our money unit, we then walk to the nearby store (with lots of parent helpers) and spend the dollar.

Before our trip, I send home a permission slip for parents to sign; on it they can list any items their child is NOT allowed to buy, such as gum or soda. I inform the store of our trip in advance. During the trip, the children have to count out their money at the counter and pay by themselves (of course, help is there if needed). It takes a while for everyone to finish, but it's a worthwhile activity!

Participate in estimation activities

Idea: Find a small clear plastic jar with a lid. Send it home with one child each week to fill it up with something. Make sure the child counts the number of items he/she puts in the container and records it on a piece of paper and gives it to you. The other children then estimate how many items are in the jar by verbally telling you or by writing their guess on a strip of paper for you to see. At the end of the week, the actual number of items is revealed, and you can send home the contents of the jar in a plastic bag with the child who brought them in. Parents often fill the jar with something edible, and we enjoy a treat when we are through guessing!

Students should also be able to:

- understand some basic addition and subtraction concepts
- understand one-to-one correspondence from one to five
- develop fraction knowledge by dividing items and creating fair shares

You may find that these exit expectations are either too low or too high for your classroom, depending on the school you teach in, the prior knowledge and experience of the children in your class, and your kindergarten entrance date. Use this list as a guide and adjust it according to your own needs, curriculum requirements, first-grade expectations, and state standards.

Classroom Environment

How to Create an Instructive, Colorful, Hands-on Environment

One of the biggest decisions you need to make before the school year begins is how to set up your room. Room size and shape vary from school to school, so work with what you have. When setting up your room, it's wise to include the following areas in your design. Always remember to put books in each area.

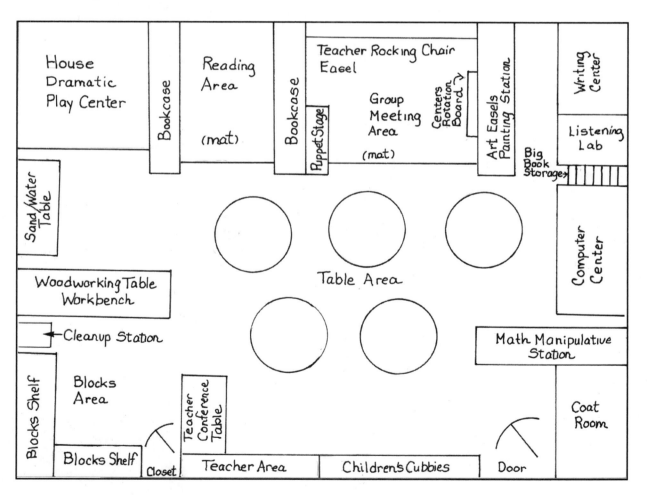

Work and Play Areas

Reading Area/Library Corner

This is a spot for the children to use for interacting with books. It should be in a corner or lined on each side with bookshelves to ensure privacy and quiet for children who choose to read there. It's important to make this area cozy and peaceful.

SUPPLIES:

Books, books, and more books!

A rug or mat to sit/lie on

A cozy blanket or quilt to curl up with

Puppets to read to

A comfortable chair

Child-size rocking chair

Some large pillows

Earphones (Use old ones from your library or media center. Cut off the cords, and the children can wear them to cut down on noise distractions.)

A lamp

Flashlights

Baskets to keep books organized

Computer Center

This is an area for stationing one or more computers. It must be located near a power source and network wiring. Children can use the computers to create pictures, type, or use computer programs.

SUPPLIES:

Computer table or long, rectangular table

Computer, monitor, and printer

Software

Appropriate-height chairs

Mouse pad

Adequate lighting

A basket of books about computers

Listening Lab

This will be a place to listen to music, songs, or books on tape.

SUPPLIES:

A tape recorder

At least four or five sets of headphones

Tapes of songs

Books with prerecorded audiotapes

SUPPLIES:

Easel

Paint pots

Paintbrushes

Paint

Old shirts or smocks

Twenty-four- by thirty-six-inch manila or white paper

Clothespins to hang the paper on the easel

A place to keep pictures to dry (a skirt hanger or a hanger for drying stockings works great)

Clothespins to hang pictures

Rubber bands to use when you roll up paintings to send home

A basket of books about artists, artwork, and/or painting

Painting Station

This is an area where one to four children can paint or create works of art. The children can put on old shirts or smocks while they use messy materials.

SUPPLIES:

Dustpan

Hand-held brush

Child-size broom

Sponges

Paper towels

A bucket

Spray bottles of water

Cleanup Station

Designate one place in the room where all the cleanup supplies are to be kept. The children can go to this station whenever they need supplies for cleaning up.

SUPPLIES:

A large rug or mat

A teacher-size rocking chair

An easel or chart stand

A blackboard

A book basket or display stand filled with books you want to read this week

Group Meeting Area

You will use this area for reading aloud to the class, group instruction, circle time, singing, reading charts, and so on. This area should be open and easily accessible to the children. It should be near a blackboard or chart stand so you can teach group lessons there.

SUPPLIES:

A table that can seat four children

Child-size chairs

Writing supplies, which can include the following:

> Notebooks
> Notepads
> Waitress pads
> Voided checks
> Bank deposit or withdrawal slips
> Index cards
> Fancy stationery
> Assorted envelopes
> Note cards
> Thank-you cards
> Postcards
> Assorted canceled stamps
> Pencils of assorted sizes
> Pencil grips
> Markers
> Crayons
> Tracing templates
> Cut-out letters
> Rubber stamps
> Stamp pads
> Letters to trace
> Clipboards
> Post-It notes
> Invitations
> Grocery lists
> Date books
> Date stamp
> Calendars
> Blank business cards
> Junk-mail applications
> Magazines
> Scissors
> Stapler
> Booklets of blank paper
> Colored paper
> Small pieces of cardbord
> Alphabet chart mounted on wall and table
> Books about authors and writing

SUPPLIES:

Rectangular or circular tables that can seat four to six children

Sturdy chairs

A basket of books on each table

Writing Center

In this area, the children have the freedom to experiment with different types of writing and different media with which to write.

Table Area

In this area, the children do seat work, writing, and art projects; have a snack; and so forth. Make sure the tables are adjusted to an appropriate height for kindergarten-age children.

SUPPLIES:

Sturdy shelves for the blocks

A set of quality wooden blocks (including an ample supply of both large and small blocks of various shapes)

Miniature cars, trucks, and other vehicles

Miniature people

Miniature road signs (available in school-supply catalogs)

Pictures of buildings in your community to mount on the wall in the blocks area

Index cards and markers to make signs for buildings

Lots of books about buildings, roads, castles, cities, and shapes

Blocks Area

Have an area where the children can create big structures and leave them up for a day or two. I allow a maximum of four children at a time in this area, and I have a strict rule that no building can be higher than a yardstick. I always have the children measure their structures to make sure they adhere to the "kindergarten building code."

It's helpful to mark the storage shelves with shapes that correspond to the shapes of the blocks. This acts as a guideline for children during cleanup; they put the blocks away by matching their shapes with the shapes on the shelves.

SUPPLIES:

Shelving with numerous inserts

Name tags to mark each child's name

Bookbinding tape to mount the name tags (and children's pictures)

Mailbox/Cubby Area

Each child needs a small, but special, place to call his/her own.

If you do not have the space or money for shelves, try putting a pillow-case on the back of each child's chair. Slide the pillowcase over the back of the chair, as if you were putting it over a pillow. Once the case edge touches the seat of the chair, roll it up, as you would a pant cuff, about eight inches, and stitch on each side.

SUPPLIES:

Clear or opaque plastic tubs with or without lids

Math manipulatives: pattern blocks, color cubes, shape blocks, Unifix cubes, counting pieces, attribute blocks, etc.

Shelves

Labels for the tubs

A basket of books about math topics or stories involving math

Math Manipulative Station

This area has shelving that is easily accessible to the children and at their level for easy retrieval of the math manipulatives. The children can use these math items during free play, too!

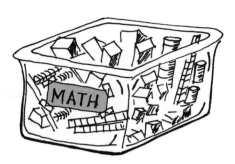

SUPPLIES:

Dress-up clothes

Kitchen supplies

Play kitchen furniture

Storage tubs

Puppets

Dolls

Fake food

Plastic kitchen utensils

Child-size table and chairs

Books about occupations, community, families, etc.

House/Dramatic Play Center

This area is for play-acting, dramatic play, and role-playing. Here the children can dress up and take on new personalities. You will see many imaginary life scenarios played out in this setting.

SUPPLIES:

Sand table/water table

Play sand (Make sure the bag of sand says that it is safe for children to use.)

Sand toys

Water toys

Measuring cups, spoons, and ladles

Books about dinosaurs, the beach, fish, water, etc.

Dustpan and hand-held broom for cleanup

Sand Table/Water Table

In this area, the children can play in either sand or water. Lots of science experiments can take place in this area as well. Two children at a time fit at my sand table. They play, measure, build, pour, and have fun with the sand or water.

SUPPLIES:

Woodworking table

Safety goggles

Child-size ball-peen hammers

Wood (Soft wood, such as pine, is best.)

Nails with large heads

Plastic or paper bags to transport finished products home

Nontoxic wood glue

Books about wood, woodworking occupations, etc.

Woodworking Table

This area is for creating things out of wood and nails. If you can't afford to buy a workbench, a large log works just as well. Position the log so that it lies flat on the floor and let the children drive nails into the top until the surface is covered with them.

Coat Room

This is an area for the children to store their coats, backpacks, and snack or lunch boxes.

SUPPLIES:

Large cubbies with hooks for coats

Shelves for backpacks and snack or lunch boxes

A basket of books that children can check out to take home or a "bring one, take one" basket (A child donates a book to the basket and takes one home.)

Teacher Area

It's good to have a place in the classroom to call your own. This space should be where you keep your desk, files, books, records, personal belongings, and daily supplies.

SUPPLIES:

Desk

An adult-size chair

Bookcase

File cabinet

Lots of professional books

A stash of mood-food (For me, it's chocolate!)

Other helpful tips to remember:

Your classroom environment will reflect a lot about you.

Don't be afraid to show your personal side. If you love plants, bring some in. If you love bright colors, get some splashy curtains, rugs, or throw pillows. Be yourself.

Keep in mind that you want to be able to see every student from anywhere in the classroom.

Avoid high shelves or interior walls that will hamper your view of the children.

Think easy accessibility.

Create a classroom that will allow you to move easily from one area to another to avoid delays and disruptions.

Think outside the box.

Simple boxes can provide lots of storage.

- Pizza boxes stack and store nicely.
- Large appliance boxes can be cut in half to create a standing display.
- Orange construction fence netting can be hung from the ceiling to make a display area.
- One side of a refrigerator box can be hung from the ceiling to make an instant wall.
- Boxes of graduated sizes can be stacked on top of one another to make an art display station.
- A large washer/dryer box can be laid on its side to make a center. You can equip the center with a flashlight or two.

Change is good

Change things around as needed. If one design or placement is not working, change it.

I change students' table assignments every month. I redo the name tags and tape them at new seats. The day before I do this, I write a letter, together with the class, to the "Table Fairy." The children help me compose it as I write it on a piece of large chart paper. It usually reads something like this:

Dear Table Fairy,
Please change our seats tonight.
We like to sit by new friends.
Love, (each child signs his/her name)

After I change the name tags, I sprinkle a little bit of glitter on each tabletop. (This is fairy dust, of course!)

Classroom Schedules

Your class schedule will depend on whether you teach an all-day, half-day, or extended-day program. Whichever type of program you have, you should begin the day with a coming-together or group-meeting time.

Here are two schedules that I follow:

HALF DAY

8:50 – 9:00	Bus arrival, seat work, math manipulative play
9:00 – 9:10	Group meeting time
9:10 – 10:00	Reading, writing, language arts
10:00 – 10:25	Snack, centers, playtime, teacher conference time

At this time, the children can eat their snack and then proceed to their playtime activity or center choice, whichever we are doing that day. During this time I call groups of children or individuals for instruction in specific areas of need.

10:25 – 10:45	Math
10:45 – 11:20	Science/social studies/art or craft projects
11:20 – 11:30	Read aloud and pack up for dismissal
11:30	Dismissal

FULL DAY

I do not try to pack more into a full-day program; instead, I devote more time to each area.

8:50 – 9:10	Arrival, seat work, math manipulative play
9:10 – 9:25	Group meeting time
9:25 – 10:25	Reading, writing, language arts
10:25 – 11:10	Snack, centers, playtime, teacher conference time
11:10 – 11:20	Big book reading/read aloud
11:20 – 12:00	Science/social studies/art or craft projects
12:00 – 1:00	Lunch and recess
1:00 – 1:35	Math
1:35 – 2:00	Rest (some states mandate a rest period; check your school policy)
2:00 – 2:25	Reading, writing, language arts
2:25 – 2:45	Read aloud and pack up for dismissal
2:45	Dismissal

The main difference between a half-day program and a full-day program should be *time*. You should not be forced to add more curriculum or pressure children to grow and learn faster. As teachers, we know that is inappropriate and impossible anyway.

You have to work in "specials" as needed. Often you cannot request a time for these classes. You are given a time, and that's that. Some days you will just have to "rob Peter to pay Paul."

Question & Answer

What do you mean by "rob Peter to pay Paul"?

I mean that packing everything into a half-day kindergarten program is virtually impossible! If you try, you will be frustrated every day. Some days you will have to give up, say, science to concentrate on social studies and then go back to doing science the following day.

There are even some days when I don't get a chance to read aloud to the children. This is a cardinal sin for me! If I have a day like that, I pull out a favorite book and say to the children, "Don't let me start the day until I read this book to you tomorrow!" Of course, some children remind me as soon as they walk in the door the next morning. They keep me on my toes. Adjust your schedule as needed and remind yourself that you are doing the best you can with the time you have.

Bulletin Boards

Over the years I have spent countless hours working on bulletin boards by myself. But now I view bulletin boards as collaborative projects. At the beginning of the school year, all the bulletin boards in my room are blank except for background paper and an attractive border. I tell the children that these bulletin boards belong to all of us and that together we will decide what to put on them. Throughout the year we decide what will go on the bulletin boards and decorate them together.

Birthday Bulletin Board

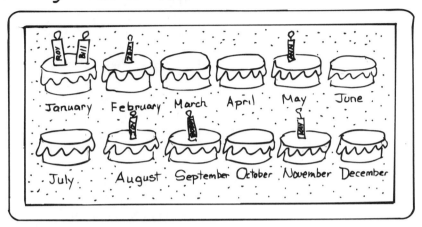

For example, one bulletin board is devoted to birthdays. We design paper birthday cakes for each month, and on the candles for each month's cake I write the names of the children who have birthdays. The children make cards, which are displayed on the board. Each child is given a card on his/her birthday. The birthday crowns for the month are also pinned up on the board, as well as any special pictures the children have created.

Calendar Bulletin Board

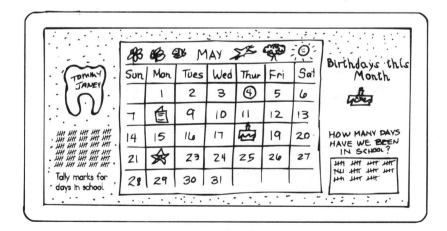

Another bulletin board is devoted to the calendar. I put up a grid for the current month, and the children make the numbers, date markers, month sign, and special day/event pictures. We count the days of school and also create charts for children who lose a tooth during the month.

Kid Stuff Bulletin Board

I have a "kid stuff " bulletin board for the children's special things. Works of art or writings that the children either bring from home or create at school are put up on this board. This gives all of us a window into each child's interests and talents. Each month I take all the papers down and store them in a three-ring binder. This becomes a favorite reading book for the class.

I have a bulletin board in the hall outside the classroom that I use for the Star of the Week. I divide it into two halves: one for the morning class and one for the afternoon class. The Star of the Week can bring in photos of himself/herself, family, friends, pets, relatives, etc., to put up on the board for this special week.

Traveling Bulletin Board

An alternative to the Star of the Week board is to have a traveling bulletin board.

This is a small, portable bulletin board that the featured child takes home on Friday and returns on Monday all decorated with pictures and treasures of his/her life. (Send thumbtacks home in a little plastic film container.)

You can devote a bulletin board to one child each week. All the other students can make a picture for that week's child to be tacked to the board. At the end of the week, you can compile the items to make a book for the child.

Organizational Bulletin Board

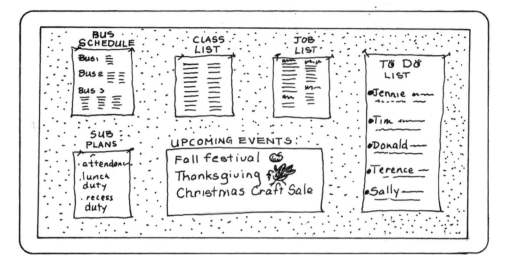

The most common use for class bulletin boards is to augment a unit of study. Use this space to place pictures, words, or items that reflect the theme you are studying. Another common use is for organizational items, such as snack orders, class lists, incentive charts, class schedules, and other items of importance. This keeps you organized at a glance.

Every school supply catalog has bulletin-board cutouts and ready-made graphics. Buy them if you like them, but remember that "kid-made" is even better!

Question & Answer

What should I do for a child who does not bring in any photographs for the Star of the Week bulletin board?

I take lots of photos during the year. I put pictures featuring that child on the bulletin board. I also have the other children draw a picture either of the Star or for the Star, and I hang them on the bulletin board. If you anticipate that this will be a problem for a particular child, wait to feature this child until you have enough photos taken of him/her in class.

Centers

The classroom areas described in the "Classroom Environment" section are permanent locations in your classroom. On the other hand, centers are temporary and constantly changing aspects of your room. They are driven by your curriculum, state standards, and theme and unit ideas.

Many teachers shy away from using centers because they feel that they do not have the time to make them or the artistic ability to create them. Don't let these concerns stop you. Instead, view centers as a way to introduce, reinforce, embellish, or extend a theme or unit of study. Just remember to start simple.

Centers should be fun

Children should *want* to go to a center. Make sure there are items in each center that can be handled, worked with, or manipulated with ease. You can make a center, called the Creation Station, that consists of a box filled with fabric scraps, staplers, yarn, paper-towel tubes, pipe cleaners, clothes hangers, tape, hole punchers, egg cartons, tissue paper, construction paper, cardboard, scissors, and any other recycled and/or free materials you can get.

Centers should relate to the course of study or curriculum needs

At a center, children should be able to learn something or extend their knowledge about a theme, unit, or curriculum area. These extension activities help to provide them with hands-on experience with the subject matter.

Center stations should be limited to five or fewer students

Three or four students is an ideal number, but you need to have enough centers to accommodate all the students in the class. You should also think about traffic flow. Have you made it easy for students to get from center to center? Have you located noisy centers away from quiet ones?

Some things that you need for setting up centers are:

- supplies (see Supply Sources on page 50)
- recycled materials (see letter on page 51)
- space for each center (Cut apart big appliance boxes for display space; you can easily fold up the sides to store them.)
- storage for center materials (Big boxes, art portfolio envelopes, expanding file folders, and plastic tubs work well.)
- a student rotation schedule or chart (I use clothespins with the children's names on them to clip onto each center's chart; see the illustration at left.)

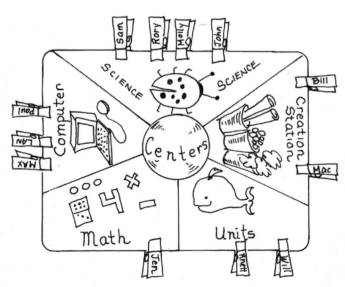

Student rotation chart

Center activities should last for ten to twenty minutes

Try to balance your centers so that the children will spend about the same amount of time at each one. Then you can rotate groups on a timed schedule.

Centers should be self-directed

Children should be able to go to a center and work independently or within a group with little or no teacher intervention. You will have to demonstrate how to use the center at first, but then the children should be self-sufficient.

Try planning your centers with colleagues or kindergarten teachers in nearby schools. You can make several centers and rotate them with other teachers. Ask parents to help with creating attractive signs for the centers or with gathering necessary supplies.

Question & Answer

What do I do about children needing help at the centers while I am trying to conference or work with another child?

I make sure that the children fully understand the directions for each center. I do this by explaining only one—or sometimes two—centers a day. I also demonstrate the activities at each center. After I am sure I've made my directions clear, I ask the children if there are any "experts" among them. These are children who completely understand how to work at a particular center and can help other children in need. I then take a twelve- by eighteen-inch piece of yellow construction paper and set it up like the sample at right:

Any child can sign his/her name on the paper. I then display it in the center. When a child comes to me for help, I read the names off the expert chart and I ask him/her to go find an expert.

I use this idea throughout the year as needs arise. For example, in the beginning of the year I make I CAN

TIE SHOES and I CAN OPEN MILK CARTONS expert charts. This saves me time, gives children opportunities to practice skills, and lets children help other children. As a child acquires a certain skill, he/she can add his/her name to the list for it. I use a ring to attach the pages together to make a "yellow pages" directory. Then anyone can let his/her fingers do the walking through our Kindergarten Yellow Pages.

Supply Sources

Creative Teaching Press
P.O. Box 6017
Cypress, CA 90630-0017
(800) 444-4287

Crystal Springs Books
75 Jaffrey Road
P.O. Box 500
Peterborough, NH 03458-0500
(800) 321-0401

The Education Center, Inc.
1607 Battleground Avenue
P.O. Box 9753
Greensboro, NC 27408
(800) 334-0298

Evan-Moor Corporation
18 Lower Ragsdale Drive
Monterey, CA 93940
(800) 777-4489

Good Apple
P.O. Box 299
Carthage, IL 62321-0299
(800) 435-7234

Lakeshore Learning Materials
2695 E. Dominguez St.
P.O. Box 6261
Carson, CA 90749
(800) 421-5354

Oriental Trading Company
P.O. Box 2318
Omaha, NE 68103-2318
(800) 228-0475

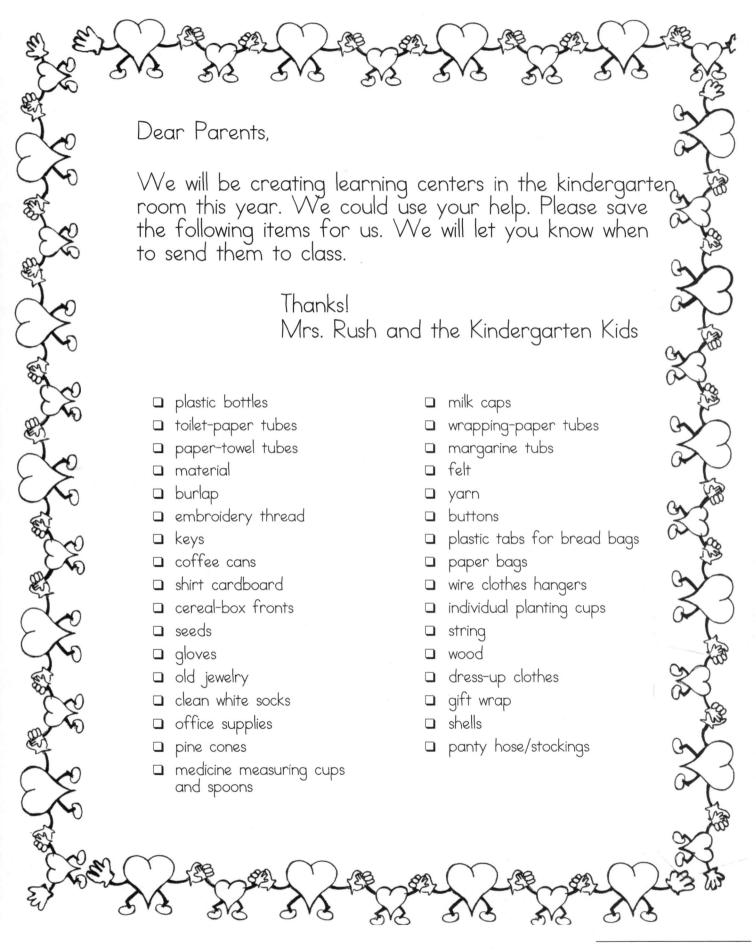

Dear Parents,

We will be creating learning centers in the kindergarten room this year. We could use your help. Please save the following items for us. We will let you know when to send them to class.

Thanks!
Mrs. Rush and the Kindergarten Kids

- ❏ plastic bottles
- ❏ toilet-paper tubes
- ❏ paper-towel tubes
- ❏ material
- ❏ burlap
- ❏ embroidery thread
- ❏ keys
- ❏ coffee cans
- ❏ shirt cardboard
- ❏ cereal-box fronts
- ❏ seeds
- ❏ gloves
- ❏ old jewelry
- ❏ clean white socks
- ❏ office supplies
- ❏ pine cones
- ❏ medicine measuring cups and spoons

- ❏ milk caps
- ❏ wrapping-paper tubes
- ❏ margarine tubs
- ❏ felt
- ❏ yarn
- ❏ buttons
- ❏ plastic tabs for bread bags
- ❏ paper bags
- ❏ wire clothes hangers
- ❏ individual planting cups
- ❏ string
- ❏ wood
- ❏ dress-up clothes
- ❏ gift wrap
- ❏ shells
- ❏ panty hose/stockings

Getting Started

Below are some tips for planning and setting up the centers in your classroom.

- Use a Centers Planning Sheet (see reproducible on page 54).
- Make a schedule/rotation board.
- Gather supplies.
- Set up materials.

- Teach the children how to use the center and how to clean up.
- Demonstrate appropriate voice volume, how to care for materials, and proper behavior in a center.

- State the objective of each center to the students and make sure they understand how that center connects to the unit of study.

A sample of the Centers Planning Sheet

Centers Planning Sheet

Unit/Theme *Insects*   Date *November, '99*

Supplies *Giant plastic bugs, magnifying glasses, bug antenna, puzzles, song charts, pipe cleaners, puff balls, goggle-eyes*

Help Needed
*① Ask second-grade teachers for microscope to borrow.
② Ask 2 parents to help with bug assembly*

Directions to Remember *When making "Izzy the Insect," remember to cut pipe cleaners small for the antennae.*

Where is it stored? *In the box marked "Insects" on the top shelf of closet.*

Introduce one center at a time

Introduce one (or sometimes two) centers a day until you explain all of them. After I have introduced the different centers in my classroom, I review the directions and begin the rotations.

Don't forget that your permanent classroom areas can be used for centers, too

Try making your sand table into a dinosaur-fossil-hunting station. Your writing center can be a station for making books about your current theme. The blocks area can serve as the community-mapping station.

Get help!

Parents are a great resource of help with centers, whether it be by collecting supplies or creating graphics. Encourage the children to do the same. Also encourage the children to add to a center with items of their own. (Make rules that protect a child's personal belongings.)

Keep an eye on things

Sometimes a center just does not work: The children get a project done in record time and end up milling around the room looking for something else to do. Don't be afraid to revise your plan for a particular center.

Don't pressure yourself to have your centers look like Walt Disney World

Start with one center and try it out. Pick a subject area that is of personal interest and significance to you. Kindergarten children love centers, and it is well worth the effort it takes to create them.

Use center time to conference with individual children

While the children are actively working at their center activities, you can get some time to conference with one child or with a small group of children. The understanding is that you've explained the directions for the centers, and all the children know what to do and where to go for each center.

Question & Answer

How can I protect a child's belongings if he/she brings them into school to be included in a center activity?

Use the dot method. Put red sticker dots on items that cannot be touched (or must be handled with extra-special care), and put green sticker dots on things that can be touched, played with, or manipulated. I have found that this method works well and that the children are very respectful of each other's treasures.

Here are a few additional pointers:

Centers Planning Sheet

Unit/Theme:_____ Date:_____

Supplies: _____

_____

_____

Help Needed:_____

_____

_____

Directions to Remember:_____

_____

_____

Where Is It Stored?_____

_____

_____

Addressing Standards with Centers

Each state in the U.S. has its own set of standards for education. Curriculums around the country are rewritten, revisited, and revised based on these standards. Your school should have copies of your state's standards for your use, review, and implementation. You can also obtain copies from your state education office. To obtain national standards, visit the Web site http://www.mcrel.org/standards-benchmarks. These national standards cover grades K–12. You should look under the K–2 or K–4 category to find kindergarten requirements. You can also do a Web search for educational standards for your state.

As you read your state's standards, check them for specific wording and details. After reviewing these documents, you can use your classroom center time to implement, augment, and comply with the standards. What follows is a brief rundown of how the centers in my classroom address various national standards.

My **reading center** is set up with books and a variety of print. This aligns with Language Arts Standard 5, Grades K–2: *Demonstrates competence in the general skills and strategies of the reading process. Understands that print conveys meaning.* As I instruct the children in the use of the reading center, introduce new books that I put in the center, and interact with the children while they are reading in the center, I am complying with this standard.

In my **listening lab center,** I set up a tape recorder, headsets, books with stories on tape, and tapes with songs, rhymes, and chants. This aligns with the Language Arts Standard 8, Grades K–2: *Demonstrates competence in speaking and listening as tools for learning. Listens to and recites familiar stories, poems, and rhymes with patterns.* I teach songs, rhymes, and stories during the day, and these are reintroduced and reinforced in the listening center.

My **writing center** contains all the tools necessary for composing and delivering a written message. This center aligns with Language Arts Standard 1, Grades K–2: *Demonstrates competence in the general skills and strategies of the writing process.* The instruction I provide for using the center covers the standards requirements, and I demonstrate writing during mini-lessons and weekly journal-writing time.

 My **math manipulative** center, which contains manipulatives, pattern blocks, tiles, and materials that can be used to demonstrate mathematical/problem-solving activities, aligns with Mathematics Standard 1, Grades K–2: *Uses a variety of strategies in the problem-solving process. Uses whole-number models (e.g., pattern blocks, tiles, or other manipulative materials) to represent problems.* You can set up simple problems, patterns to copy, and tangram models in a center like this in your classroom.

My **science table/center,** which contains weather calendars, a water table, and hands-on science items, aligns with Science Standard 1, Grades K–2: *Understands basic features of the Earth.* This standard stresses the knowledge of weather; seasonal changes; and solid, liquid, and gas properties.

My **blocks center** contains not only building blocks but also pictures of our neighborhood, community, and school. This aligns with Geography Standard 2, Grades K–2: *Knows the location of places, geographic features, and patterns of the environment. Knows the location of school, home, neighborhood, community, state, and country.* The children can build and label various buildings that they see all around their world.

My **woodworking center,** with its hammers, nails, screwdriver, glue, and wood, aligns with Life Work Standard 1, Grades K–2: *Makes effective use of basic tools.* This standard deals with children's using hammers, nails, and other tools to demonstrate an understanding of their use and function.

My **painting center** aligns with Visual Arts Standard 5, Grades K–2: *Understands the characteristics and merits of one's own artwork and the artwork of others.* The children learn to appreciate their own artistic efforts as well as those of their classmates.

My **computer center** aligns with Technology Standard 1, Grades K–2: *Knows the characteristics and uses of computer hardware and operating systems.* The children experiment with different computer hardware and software in this center.

My **housekeeping center** aligns with Working with Others Standard 4, Grades K–2: *Displays effective interpersonal communication skills.*

My **puppet center,** which stresses displaying friendliness to others, using emotions to convey thoughts, making eye contact when speaking, and communicating with others in a clear manner, also aligns with this standard.

Assessment

Assessment should begin with the introductory visits you make to students' homes before the school year begins. I do not, however, do any formal assessments on the children until they come to school on the first day. It is important to get as many baseline samples of the children's work as soon as possible. If you wait to begin your assessment process until the end of the first month of the school year or later, you will miss a great opportunity to show the children, their parents, and yourself the tremendous growth kindergartners make each day, week, and month.

You should always formulate your goals first and then plan your assessments accordingly. Once you have established what it is that you want a particular student to learn, you should ask yourself, "What evidence will convince me that the child has mastered this skill?"

It is best to design your assessment before you teach the related task. Thoroughly think through what results you are after. Try to think backward from your goal: Identify the steps that are necessary to take for a child to reach the goal. Make sure that these steps are clear to both you and the child.

Make each step filled with success. This means if a student has trouble with a concept or task, break down the task into smaller bits so the child can experience success with each part of the task. For example, if I am assessing a child's knowledge of the alphabet and he/she does not recognize any letters, I show the child his/her name and ask the child to tell me the letters in it. (This is something that most every child knows.) Then I tell the child that he/she DOES know letters! Success leads to more success.

Students will gain from the assessment process only if there is immediate positive or constructive feedback. As the old saying goes, "If you don't tell a child where he/she is going, anyplace will do!" Let the children hear you think out loud: State what you want them to learn, and explain how they will go about learning it.

Monthly Assessment Schedule

Your assessments should be used to enhance both your teaching and the students' learning. As a teacher, you can redesign your instruction to fit a particular child's needs or learning style based on the results of the assessment. Think of assessment as a tool for you to use to revamp your lessons, strategies, and methods of instruction.

It is very helpful to set up a month-to-month schedule for your assessments. See the one below.

Monthly Assessment Schedule	SEPT.	OCT.	NOV.	DEC.	JAN.	FEB.	MARCH	APRIL	MAY/JUNE
Draw a person/draw yourself	X			X			X		X
Draw a tree	X			X			X		X
Write all the letters you know	X								X
Number writing from 1–30	X		X		X				X
Alphabet letter/sound checklist	X		X		X		X		X
Number recognition from 1–30	X			X			X		
Sample journal entry	X	X	X	X	X	X	X	X	X
Counting (How high can the student count?)		X					X		
Dictated sentence: "*The red cat is old.*"					X				X
Rhyming word assessment		X				X		X	X
Write all the words you know						X			X
Sight word/short vowel test						X			X
Write your name	X		X		X				X

If your school year starts in August and ends in May, you should adjust this schedule accordingly.

By the end of the school year, the kindergarten child should know the following:

1. The letters of the alphabet by sight.

2. The sounds of at least three-quarters of the alphabet, excluding *y, x, q,* and *w*.

3. How to say a word that rhymes with a word you say.

4. How to write in a journal.

5. Some sight words (e.g., like, love, mom, dad, we, I, me, the).

6. How to write his/her first and last name.

7. How to write numbers to thirty.

8. How to count by rote to thirty.

9. How to make an ABABAB pattern with colored blocks.

10. How to sort and classify items by attributes.

11. How to add and subtract simple numbers with the help of manipulatives.

12. How to identify a penny, nickel, and dime.

13. How to tell time to the hour.

14. How to count by twos to ten, by fives to fifty, and by tens to 100.

15. How to use scissors, crayons, markers, and pencils correctly.

16. How to sit and listen to a story.

17. How to predict what comes next in a story based on prior information.

18. How to picture-read a book.

19. Where text is located on a book page.

20. Capital and lowercase letters.

21. Marks of punctuation.

22. How to communicate using full sentences.

23. How to use the bathroom independently.

Feel free to add more to this list or revise it to make it suitable for your particular group of kindergarten children.

Alphabet Letter/Sound Checklist

Use the assessment on page 61 to obtain specific information about which letters and sounds each child in your class knows. You can then use this information as a basis for each child's instruction.

Do this assessment individually. Early in the first month of the school year, sit with the child so that you can both look at the page together. Using a colored pen, put the date at the top of the page. You then ask the child to name each letter and make the letter's sound. If he/she recognizes the letter, put a check mark in the appropriate box, using the same color of ink that you used to write the date. If the child can produce the correct sound, check that box, using the same color of ink. Do this for the entire alphabet. You may want to draw a line to split a box into two parts if you want the child to produce two sounds for certain letters, such as the hard and soft sounds for the letters *c* and *g*.

In November, take a different-colored pen and check off the responses that the child now knows. It's unnecessary to go through the letters/sounds that the child knew on the previous assessment. Date the paper with the same colored pen. In January, use a third colored pen (different than what you used the first two times) to mark the letters/sounds that the child now knows. In March, use a fourth colored pen.

Using a different color of ink each time you assess lets you tell at a quick glance what the child knew at each assessment conference. Thus, you can clearly see the growth the child has made. Pens that have four different-colored ink barrels are handy to use for this assessment.

Keep doing the same assessment page every two months until the child successfully knows all the letters and sounds. For some children, this will be the first day they enter school; for others, it may not even be on the last day. Everyone else, of course, will fall somewhere in between.

Use the reproducible form on page 62 to inform the parent(s)/guardian(s) about which letters they can help their child learn at home.

Alphabet Assessment

Letter	Sound	Letter	Sound	Letter	Sound
Bb		Mm		Oo	ŏ / ō
Ss		Qq		Ww	
Zz		Xx		Aa	ă / ā
Dd		Ee		Hh	ĕ / ē
Cc	s / k	Ii		Yy	ĭ / ī
Tt		Jj		Gg	g / j
Kk		Ll		Nn	
Vv		Rr		Ff	
Pp		Uu	ŭ / ū	Name: _____ Date: _____	

Comments: _____

Dear_____

These are the letters of the alphabet that
I need help with:

All the others I know by sight! Aren't you
proud of me?

Love,

Reproducible

Writing Fluency Checklist

Use copies of this checklist to record your observations of two or three students at a time while they write in their journals. The checklist will enable you to check off a lot of information quickly as you observe the students' writing behavior (e.g., looking around the room for a resource to find out how to spell a word). The boxes that remain empty next to a child's name will show you what you need to work on with that child during a one-on-one conference or small-group session.

Student Name: _____

WRITING FLUENCY CHECKLIST

Date Checked:	Sept.	Nov.	Jan.	March
Draws picture				
Draws picture and tells about it				
Scribbles				
Writes print-like symbols				
Labels pictures				
Uses environmental print				
Writes one/few letter(s)				
Writes letters to match picture				
Uses some letter/sound knowledge				
Can read back own writing				
Begins to leave spaces between words				
Writes first letter of words				
Writes first and last letter of words				
Uses some medial sounds				
Uses capital letters to begin sentence				
Uses punctuation				
Uses resources to help with spelling				
Shows knowledge of sense of a sentence				
Writes a sentence				

Journal Entry/Writing Stages

You can make journal-writing a monthly assessment by photocopying a page out of each child's journal to document his/her writing growth. Some of the levels of writing that you will see are listed below. Included are student samples that illustrate each of these writing stages.

Picture writing

The child draws a picture to get his/her meaning across to the reader.

Curlicue writing

This writing is scribbled from left to right and follows a stream of consciousness communicated verbally by the child. The child can "read" his/her message to you. But once when I asked a child to read back his curlicue writing to me, he responded, "Mrs. Rush, you know I can't read cursive yet!"

Symbol writing

This writing is filled with print-like symbols that might look like letters, numbers, or shapes. The child can "read" his/her writing to you.

Unrelated letters

At this stage, the child realizes that writing is made up of letters. This writing consists of a string of letters that the child knows how to write, but it does not spell anything or relate to the sounds of the words the child wants to communicate.

Name writing

Often the first word a child learns to write is his/her name. At this stage, he/she will use it to label every picture.

Consonants

The child can hear the dominant letter sounds in the words he/she wants to write. Usually the writing consists of the beginning and ending consonant sounds of the words.

Familiar words/sight words

The child can write words from memory, such as *cat, mom, dad,* and *dog.*

Vowel sounds

The child begins to insert vowels into words and realizes that a word cannot be a word without a vowel.

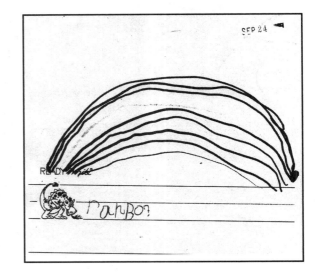

Sentence writing

The child can communicate by writing a single sentence to convey a thought.

Story writing

The child uses several sentences to make up a story.

Santa and reindeer

First page of story

Santa is saying Ho-Ho-Ho-Ho-Ho-Ho, Ho-Ho-Ho

Second page of story

Sentence Dictation

G ive this test to students at the midway point of the school year and again at the end of the year. You can give the test individually or to the whole class. Make sure you date all the papers. Say the sentence "The red cat is old." Have the children repeat it after you. Then tell them to try to write as much of the sentence as they can. You can repeat it as many times as you feel the children need to hear it in order to write it.

Sentence Dictation   Date:_____

This child does not know any letters or sounds, but he/she has an understanding that you write something on paper to convey a thought. This child also knows that print goes across a line from left to right. I would teach this child alphabet letters, beginning with the letters in his/her name.

Sentence Dictation   Date:_____

This child knows that letters, shapes, and numbers carry meaning, but he/she is getting them all confused. I would teach this child alphabet letter recognition, beginning with the letters in his/her name. I would then compare and contrast the letters of the alphabet with shapes and numbers so this child could see the differences and/or similarities among them.

Sentence Dictation   Date:_____

This child knows some letters in addition to the letters of his/her name, which are written in the middle of this string of letters. I would teach this child the letters of the alphabet and letter sounds, beginning with consonants and then moving to vowels. Consonant sounds are easier to hear and produce than short vowel sounds.

This child is just beginning to orally distinguish some sounds of letters as well as sounds in words. Notice the *V* for *the*, *D* for *red*, *T* for *cat*, and *O* for *old*. I would continue to teach this child how to sound out words slowly in order to hear the individual sounds in them. This child is ready to hear and write the beginning and ending consonants in words. I would review all alphabet letters for recognition and teach this child all corresponding letter sounds.

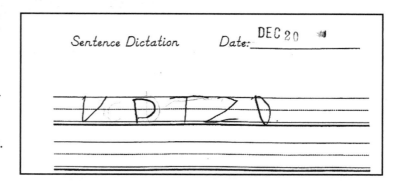

This child is beginning to experiment with writing full words and hearing sounds in a word. I would work on segmenting words so he/she could identify each letter sound in a word. I would also teach him/her sight words needed for writing, such as *the, is, and, like,* and *love*. This child understands that there are spaces between words and that sentences end with a mark of punctuation.

The dots on the paper are what I call "reminder dots." I teach the children to put two fingers next to the right of the word they just finished writing. They then touch the word they just finished with the pencil point, hop their pencil over their two fingers, and put a very small dot on the page to the right of their fingers. This is their reminder dot, which tells them where to start writing the next word in the sentence.

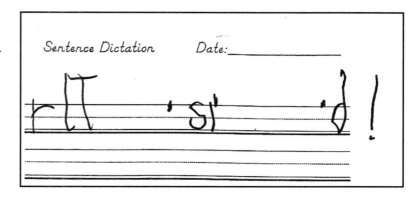

This child has a lot of knowledge about letters, sounds, and words but is weak with short vowel sounds. I would teach this child the short and long vowel sounds and medial sounds in words.

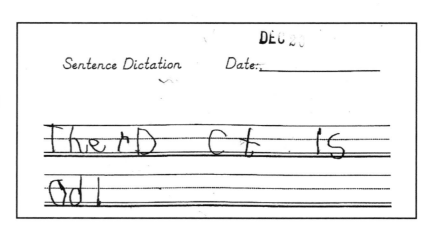

Sentence Dictation   Date:_____

The
red
cat
is
OLD
I

This child has a well-developed knowledge of letters, sounds, and words. He/she needs help with horizontal writing skills and the knowledge that print goes from left to right across a line and loops to the next line. I would present books to this child and have him/her track the print across the line with a finger and loop down to the next line. I would also work with this child during journal-writing time, showing him/her how to write words across the page and leave spaces between words rather than skip to the next line after each word.

Sentence Dictation   Date:_____

The Red cat is
old.

This child is ready to move to a higher level of reading and writing. I would provide him/her with books that have more than one line of print and teach him/her journal-writing of stories with two sentences or more to describe a picture.

Anecdotal Records

Anecdotal records consist of comments you write while observing children throughout the day, supported with examples of the children's work. You can write your comments in short phrases, long sentences, or whatever style of writing with which you feel most comfortable. Just make sure you don't use a code that you can't figure out or read back at the end of the day.

The purpose of anecdotal records is to document what you observe while you are "kid watching." You are looking for and documenting your students' growth in a natural setting. The children are engrossed in their work, and you are the keen observer. You can then share your notes anytime you need to.

I keep note pads, index cards, and pencils at strategic places around my classroom so that I can grab them anytime I notice something I want to write down. I then read over my notes at the end of the day and file them in my students' work folders or files.

Another note-taking method is to use a loose-leaf notebook containing a blank piece of paper for each child with his/her name at the top. You simply flip to a child's page and record your information whenever you observe something. Be sure you date each entry.

Another method is to use sticky labels. Take a clipboard around the room with you so you have a surface to write on. Write your observations on the sticky notes and attach them to the clipboard when you are done. Then put the notes in each child's file folder.

I tape index cards together in an overlapping fashion so that I have a "flip chart" that lets me quickly access each child's card with a flick of the wrist. I use color-coded index cards: blue for reading, yellow for writing, and pink for math. You can use other colors for other curriculum areas.

The reproducible Student Observation Form on the next page makes it easy to observe five students per day and keep your notes all on one page. This method helps you ensure that you observe all the students in your class by the end of the week. When you are finished note-taking, simply cut apart the page and put the individual sections in each child's portfolio or file.

Some teachers use standardized checklists, but these are useful only when they reflect the aspects of the curriculum that you want to observe. Anecdotal records, on the other hand, are individualized by you for your students. They let you record only what you value. The notes you take help you get to know each of your students better. In addition, reading the notes will guide your teaching for the whole group, for small groups, and for individuals.

Student Observation Form

Student's Name: _Connie_   Date: _10/2_
Subject Observed: _Reading_

Good book handling skills. Still needs help with letter sounds.

Student's Name: _Kaitlyn_   Date: _10/2_
Subject Observed: _Reading_

She is ready to move to harder books; can match text/oral word for word.

Student's Name: _Morgan_   Date: _10/2_
Subject Observed: _Reading_

Really identifying letters well. Needs to recognize Q, Y, U, and U.

Student's Name: _Taylor_   Date: _10/3_
Subject Observed: _Math_

Super job at patterning with Unifix cubes! Did an ABC ABC ABC pattern.

Student's Name: _Mackensie_   Date: _10/3_
Subject Observed: _Math_

Really understanding concepts better. Worked on patterning today. She is really getting it now.

Student Observation Form

Student's Name:_____   Date:_____

Subject Observed:_____

Student's Name:_____   Date:_____

Subject Observed:_____

Student's Name:_____   Date:_____

Subject Observed:_____

Student's Name:_____   Date:_____

Subject Observed:_____

Student's Name:_____   Date:_____

Subject Observed:_____

Number Writing

During the first week of the school year, have the children fill in as many numbers as they know on this form (see the reproducible on page 78). This will show you which children know how to write their numbers and which do not. It will also show you which numbers your students reverse most often. Use this information to plan your teaching strategies.

I teach a number-writing/number-recognition unit in October, so in November I use the same form to reassess the entire class. Those who still cannot form the numbers correctly need reteaching, review, and/or reinforcement.

Use this form again in January and May, noting the children who still need reteaching, review, and reinforcement each time. On pages 76 and 77 are a few samples from students in my class.

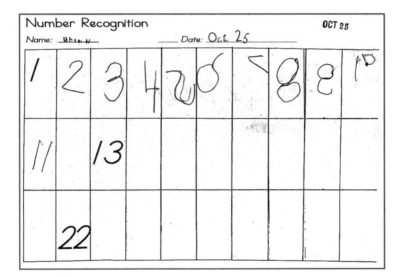

Number Recognition

I use the form on page 79 for one-on-one assessment of number recognition. It's easy to use: Show the form to the child and circle all the numbers that the child recognizes. Use the results from this test to plan number-recognition lessons both for the class and for individuals who need extra help with this skill.

Administer this test at the beginning of the school year, again in December, and a third time in March for those children who don't recognize all the numbers when you test in December.

The following sequence of number-recognition tests follows one child's progression throughout the school year.

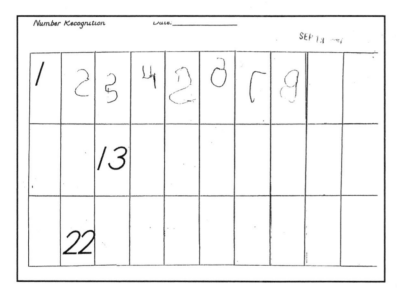

Based on the initial assessment given in mid-September, I began teaching this child a math unit concentrating on writing numbers, recognizing numbers, and counting with the class.

This assessment, from late October, shows improvement in the child's formation of numbers. He still needs practice forming the numbers 5, 6, 7, 8, and 9. At this point I began to teach him the numbers from 11 through 20.

Much improvement can be seen on this test (from mid-January) with regard to number formation, but some reversals still exist. At this point I provided the child with more number-writing practice and taught him the numbers from 20 through 30.

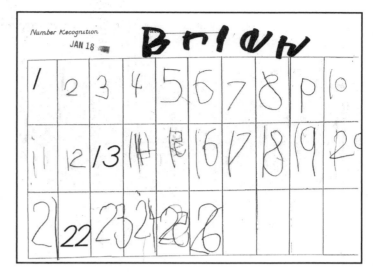

After the child completed this test in early May, I retaught him proper directionality of numbers and provided him with practice writing the numbers through 30.

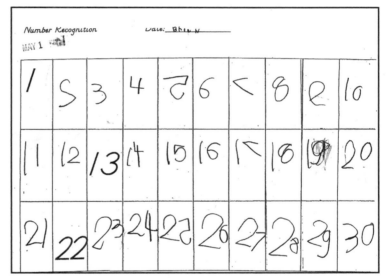

A great ending of the year! The results of this test, taken in mid-June, show that patience, reteaching, and hard work have paid off.

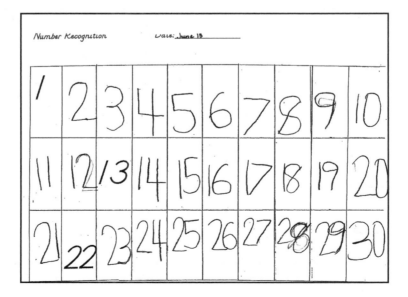

Number Recognition—Written

Name: _____ Date: _____

	13	
		22
1		

Number Recognition

Name: _____ Date: _____

2	9	4	3	1
15	5	10	16	7
17	13	11	18	8
19	22	30	6	24
21	27	12	25	20
26	28	14	29	23

Draw a Tree

G iving this test to your students on their first day of kindergarten enables you to look at their drawings and obtain an instant view of their academic and maturational levels. I adapted this idea from a drawing activity I did a few years ago. There is a high correlation among the ability to draw a tree, the academic skills a child possesses, and his/her maturational age.

You can give this test to the whole class at once if you like. It is best to separate the children so that they don't copy ideas from each other. To administer this test, give each child a blank piece of paper. Provide fat and thin crayons, washable markers, and different sizes of pencils, and let each child choose what he/she wants to use. Then tell the children to draw a tree.

Always remember to date the papers. I use a date stamp for this purpose: Simply roll the month and day on the stamp to the appropriate date, press the stamp on an ink pad, and date the children's papers with it. Date stamps are available at any stationery supply store.

I assess the draw-a-tree test results on a rubric as follows:

Level 1: This tree looks like a lollipop with one stick and a ball or some similar shape on the top. It bears very little resemblance to a tree. This level is the lowest in terms of skills and maturity.

Level 2: This tree looks like two sticks with a ball on top. There is little or no proportion to the tree. This level indicates that the child has some skills but is lacking in most areas.

Level 3: This tree has some dimension to it, along with some variations of the trunk and foliage. This is considered to be the benchmark level: A child at this level has the basic knowledge and background experiences required for him/her to best be able to achieve the kindergarten curriculum standards—and possibly go beyond them.

Level 4: This tree is elaborate in design and has lots of extras, such as an owl hole in the trunk, roots at the bottom, leaves, and extra branches. This child most likely already excels academically and socially and will continue to make great strides throughout the kindergarten year.

This assessment is not designed for tracking your students or putting them in regimented academic groups. Rather, it is intended to give you a quick picture on the first day of where most of them stand academically and maturationally. In addition, this test helps you get to know your students early on without imposing on them an academic task or assessment that may frustrate them. As you do more assessments with the children during the year, you will find that their results match those of the draw-a-tree test.

Examples of Level 1

Examples of Level 2

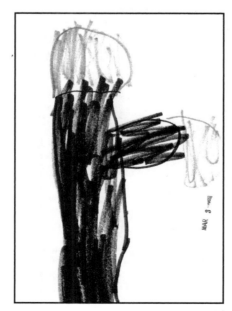

Examples of Level 3

Examples of Level 4

 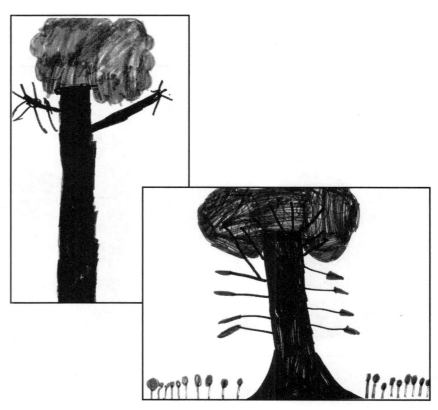

Draw a Person/Draw Yourself

This test is as simple as the draw-a-tree test and can be given to your students during the first few days of school. To administer this test, give each child a blank piece of paper. Offer a variety of drawing tools for the students to choose from. Then tell the class to draw themselves. Do not coach the children about what to draw.

You need to be careful while giving this test if you suspect you have any students with low self-esteem. Some behaviors that such a child exhibits include never looking at you, seeming to be sad all the time, or saying that things are "too hard" or that he/she "isn't good enough." If you tell these children to draw themselves, their low self-esteem may be reflected in their drawings, and therefore the drawings will not show their true abilities. When you believe you have children with low self-esteem in your class, tell the class to draw a person.

While evaluating the students' drawings, pay close attention to the different features that are drawn on the body. These include the following:

- head
- eyelashes
- ears
- nose
- hair
- neck
- arms
- five fingers
- feet
- shoes

- eyes
- eyebrows
- earrings
- mouth
- hair accessories (bows, barrettes, etc.)
- body
- hands
- legs
- toes
- other individual features

I assess the draw-a-person/draw-yourself test results on a rubric as follows. (See the sample drawings for each of these levels on the following pages.)

Level 1 drawings look the least like a person; they have a minimum of body features and parts.

Level 2 drawings look a bit more like a person but still lack lots of crucial elements.

Level 3 is the benchmark, or emergent, level. These drawings look like a person and include most of the large body parts.

Level 4 drawings have some, most, or all of the extras listed above. These drawings are very mature depictions of a person.

For further reading about this test, consult *The ABC Inventory: To Determine Kindergarten and School Readiness* by Normand Adair and George Blesch. To obtain a copy of this report, contact Educational Studies and Development, 1942 Furhman, Muskegon, MI 49441.

Examples of Level I

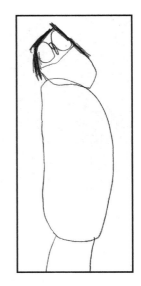

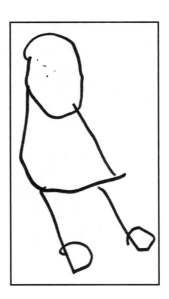

Examples of Level 2

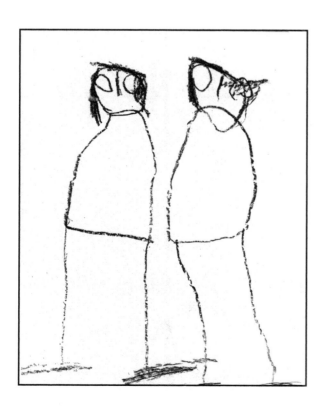

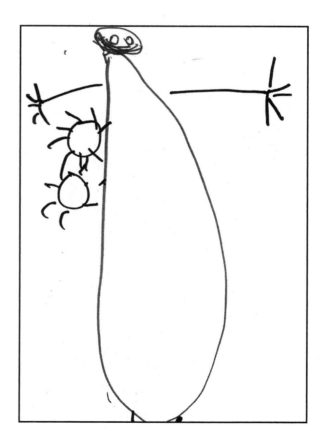

Examples of Level 3

Examples of Level 4

Word-Rhyming Test

The ability to detect rhyme in words is a good predictor of early reading success. Rhyming ability is a black-and-white issue: A child either can or cannot rhyme. There are no gray areas. When I give this test, I expect a median score of fourteen or fifteen correct out of twenty; this is a passing grade. By "passing," I mean that attaining this score indicates a child is well on the way to understanding rhyming words. A child who has a score of thirteen or lower is in need of teacher intervention and direct instruction about how words rhyme and how to listen for rhyme. This instruction is a good place to add nursery rhymes, rhyming books, and songs to your teaching routine. Children who get a low score on the word-rhyming test will clearly benefit from this kind of instruction as well as from phonological awareness training.

I give this test to each student individually. It takes about three to four minutes per child to administer. To prepare a child for this test, I explain to him/her how rhyming words work. I say something like this: "Rhyming words are words that sound the same at the end, like *peg* and *leg, net* and *set*, and *can* and *ran*. Not all words rhyme.

"Let's try some together. Does *tree* rhyme with *bee?* Yes! Why? Because *tree* and *bee* end with the same sound of *ee*. Does *block* rhyme with *sand?* No! Why? Because *block* ends with *ock*, and *sand* ends with *and*.

"Let's try some more. You tell me if these words rhyme."

Use the reproducible on the next page to administer this test.

Word-Rhyming Test

1. cat/hat

2. head/bed

3. farm/cow

4. see/me

5. bird/nest

6. night/light

7. come/home

8. seat/beat

9. beach/peach

10. warm/cold

11. flower/tower

12. mouse/house

13. watch/glove

14. hand/sand

15. day/say

16. cake/make

17. puzzle/game

18. boy/toy

19. play/ball

20. moon/soon

Score: _____/20

Sight-Word Test

This test, given toward the middle of the school year, assesses students' proficiency with beginning and ending sounds of words, medial short-vowel sounds, and some sight words that are common in a kindergarten-age child's speaking and writing vocabulary. You can give this test individually or to the whole class. (Use the reproducible form on page 91.) The completed tests will clearly show you which children need instruction in the above-mentioned skills.

Use the following word list for this test:

1. me
2. cat
3. pet
4. bit
5. not
6. hut
7. is
8. mom
9. dad
10. love

For some variation in word-ending sounds, change the short-vowel words in the list to the following:

1. can
2. pen
3. bib
4. nod
5. hum

Sight-Word Test

Name:_____ Date:_____

1. _____

2. _____

3. _____

4. _____

5. _____

6. _____

7. _____

8. _____

9. _____

10. _____

Assessment Q&A

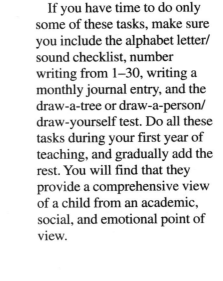

Q: **Does each assessment task have to be done on an individual basis?**

A: No! Only a few of the assessment tasks in this chapter need to be done individually. When I give the whole class an assessment, I have the children spread out to various parts of the room so that they can do their own work rather than copy someone else's. After I pass out the papers, everyone works at his/her own pace. I stress that it needs to be quiet in the room while bright minds are working.

Q: **Can I have a parent or an aide do the individual assessment tasks with the children?**

A: You can have an aide do them, but I strongly discourage it. You are the one who needs to know the children completely. If you do the assessment tasks, you will have a mental record as well as a written one of what each child can do. You will be able to remember how a particular child arrived at an answer, as well as other needs, strengths, or weaknesses that child displays. You should avoid having a parent do any assessing for you. There are many other ways in which parents can help in the classroom. (See Chapter 5, "Parents as Partners.")

Q: **What do I do with all the assessment papers the children complete?**

A: I date all the papers when I collect them. I make sure I have time to look at each paper as I file it in the folders I keep for each child. I pull these folders out and compare test results as the year progresses. I also use these papers during parent/teacher conferences to document the child's growth.

Q: **Do I have to do all the assessments?**

A: No. Pick and choose what works best for you, depending on what you want to know about your students. The standard school report card does not tell the parent or me as much as the results of these assessment tasks do. In addition, they do not take a lot of time, and they document a child's academic and maturational development and progress.

If you have time to do only some of these tasks, make sure you include the alphabet letter/sound checklist, number writing from 1–30, writing a monthly journal entry, and the draw-a-tree or draw-a-person/draw-yourself test. Do all these tasks during your first year of teaching, and gradually add the rest. You will find that they provide a comprehensive view of a child from an academic, social, and emotional point of view.

Q: **Should I be concerned only with what the child produces?**

A: No. There are three elements of assessment. One is the product component: What can the child produce? The second is the process component: How did the child get the answer, and what was the thought process used? The third is the progress component: How far has the child come since the beginning of the year? Each one of the assessments in this book will help you look at all three of these elements.

Q: **What happens when a child is clearly not ready to go on to first grade?**

A: You must anticipate this possibility early in the year and have monthly conferences with the parent(s) to discuss the child's progress. No parent will support retention if you wait until May to inform him/her of this likelihood. You have to be up front with these parents and tell them that the child is not ready—based on your assessments, observations, and professional judgment—to handle the requirements of the first-grade classroom. Because I conference every month with the parents of children who are struggling, more often than not I find that, by February, the *parent* is the one who is suggesting retention.

Retention very rarely works if the parents do not support the decision. In the past I have sent children on to first grade even though they were not ready (against my better judgment), because their parents would not support retention. I always write a letter (like the one in Chapter 8, "Dealing with Struggling Learners") and put it in the child's permanent file. I also give a copy to the parent(s), keep a copy for my files, and give copies to the principal, superintendent, and the child's first-grade teacher.

Chapter 4

Classroom Management Tips and Techniques

Whether you teach a half-day or a full-day program, you should always begin your day with a coming-together time. Teachers have various names for this: circle time, class meeting, group-share time. But regardless of what it's called, this is an important time for the children to share their thoughts, come together as a group, and establish a focus for the day. It's also an important time for you to establish the classroom climate and get a view of the children's frame of mind early in the day.

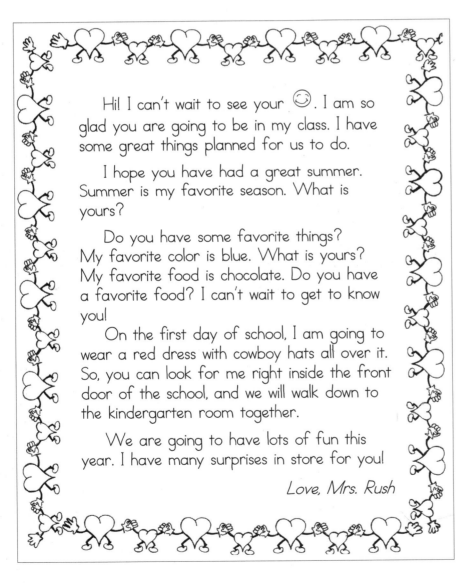

Hi! I can't wait to see your ☺. I am so glad you are going to be in my class. I have some great things planned for us to do.

I hope you have had a great summer. Summer is my favorite season. What is yours?

Do you have some favorite things? My favorite color is blue. What is yours? My favorite food is chocolate. Do you have a favorite food? I can't wait to get to know you!

On the first day of school, I am going to wear a red dress with cowboy hats all over it. So, you can look for me right inside the front door of the school, and we will walk down to the kindergarten room together.

We are going to have lots of fun this year. I have many surprises in store for you!

Love, Mrs. Rush

Sample letter for the children

The Before and After

You should start setting up your routine and schedule for the year before the children enter the classroom on the first day. Sending a letter home during the summer is a good way to begin. One sample letter appears at left, and there is one on page 95. One is for the child. In it, you introduce yourself and help relieve some anxiety on the child's part.

The other letter is for the parents. The input I receive from this letter gives me feedback about which parents are good at assessing their own child (most of them are) and which are in denial about their child's difficulties. You can learn a lot from a parental-input letter.

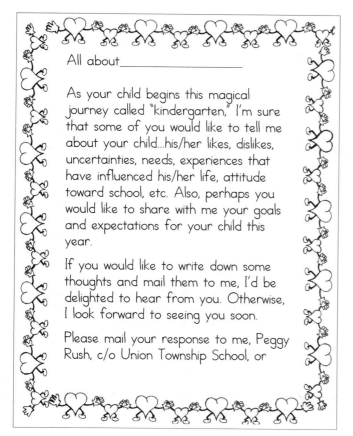

All about_____

As your child begins this magical journey called "kindergarten," I'm sure that some of you would like to tell me about your child...his/her likes, dislikes, uncertainties, needs, experiences that have influenced his/her life, attitude toward school, etc. Also, perhaps you would like to share with me your goals and expectations for your child this year.

If you would like to write down some thoughts and mail them to me, I'd be delighted to hear from you. Otherwise, I look forward to seeing you soon.

Please mail your response to me, Peggy Rush, c/o Union Township School, or

feel free to send it in with your child in September. You can include a picture of your child, if you wish. The school's address is 165 Perryville Rd., Hampton, NJ 08827.

Some things I'd like for you to know about _____are:

_____

_____

_____

_____

_____

Sample letter for parents

You can also include information on a question-and-answer sheet, using the following format.

How will I find my teacher on the first day?

Mrs. Rush will be waiting right inside the front door of the school. She will be wearing a red dress with cowboy hats on it. You will be wearing your name tag, and she will find you.

Where will I hang my coat and backpack?

Right when you walk into the classroom, there will be hooks and cubbies for your coat and backpack.

How will I know where to sit?

There will be a table that has your name on it. You can sit in that seat.

Where do I put my snack money and papers from home?

There will be a big blue basket on Mrs. Rush's desk. All your notes from home will go in there.

General Ideas

Model, Model, Model

No one model of a classroom fits every teacher's needs. First ask yourself what you want to accomplish and then formulate a routine that will foster that end. Remember this chant throughout the year: model, model, model! Whatever you want the children to learn or do, model it. Responsibility for organization cannot fall on the shoulders of the children, who have no such prior experience.

For example, as I introduce play centers in the beginning of the school year, I go to the blocks center and build a structure, take it all apart, and put the blocks back on the appropriate shelves. All the time while I am doing this, I think out loud so the children can hear me while they watch. I never assume that a child comes to school able to clean up; I explain my expectations for the cleanup task.

Early in the year, I teach the children how to clear their tables after they eat their snack. Scooping crumbs off a table is not an easy task for young hands. I dump a few Unifix cubes on a desk or table and demonstrate how the child should put one hand under the lip of the table and use the other hand to move the "crumbs" (i.e., Unifix cubes) to the end of the table and let them fall into the open, waiting hand.

In short, model, model, model whatever routines or behaviors you want the children to use in your classroom. Monitor things from time to time to see if more modeling is necessary. Remember that, to establish good routines, modeling once is never enough!

Question & Answer

I am a new teacher. Besides knowing about the curriculum and setting up my room, what should I do to get ready for my first day?

I exercise to get ready for my first days of the school year. (After the first three days, you will feel like you have run a marathon—and you probably have!) Walk, jog, swim, bike, or engage in some other physical activity to build up your stamina.

Exercise your voice. You will talk more during the first week of teaching kindergarten than you did for the whole month prior to it. Get your voice ready. Go to a ball game and yell. Call an old friend and talk for hours. Sing loud and long.

The beginning of the school year is a busy time. For the children, it is a time of transition from being the only one (or one of a few) in a parent's eyes to being one of many in a classroom. Each child will have different needs and wants and will have plenty of things to tell you. As the children enter your room in the morning, you should be there to welcome them right at the door. You should quickly establish routines for the children that answer the following questions:

- Where will they hang their coats?

- Where will they put their backpacks?

- Where will notes from home go?

- Where do the library books belong?

- Where will the children sign in?

- Where will snack money/milk money go?

- Where is the bathroom?

If you have these details in place, you should be off to a good start. Smile and enjoy your students.

Enter and Sign In, Please

A good way to monitor the children's handwriting skills is to regularly use a sign-in sheet before class meeting. You can use lined or unlined paper for this. As the children enter the classroom at the start of the day, they sign in on individual twelve- by eighteen-inch sheets or in a notebook.

As you observe the children signing in, look for who is left-handed/right-handed, who has not yet established hand dominance, who can write their names quickly and who draws their names, who remembers to sign in without being told and who doesn't, who forms a line and who barges in, who speaks the letters out loud and who is secure with the letters, and who uses the lines on the paper and who ignores them. These observations will enable you to help each child move forward with the skills he/she needs to develop.

Keep all the sign-in pages and make a big book out of them. Make sure that you date each page. I prefer to use individual sheets of paper rather than a notebook because periodically throughout the year I can display the pages from different months next to each other. Then I have the children help me compare the different months' entries. Some things we look for include lowercase and uppercase letters, letter formation, inclusion of both first name and last name, and using lines properly (if you use lined paper).

Sing with Me

Many teachers start their class's coming-together time with the song of the month. You can teach this song at the beginning of the month and sing it each day to begin the day. Put the words of the song on a chart so the children can refer to the words during the day.

Make sure you include the words to the song in the newsletter you send home so parents can sing it along with their child at home. You can also play a recording of this song whenever you want the children to clean up what they are doing. When the children hear the song begin, they know it is time to start cleaning up. By the time the song ends, cleanup should be completed.

Question & Answer

How should I arrange the children for our class meeting or group share?

I make sure that the children are seated on a mat, rug, or something else that's comfortable and that the group is in a circle. This ensures that everyone can see everyone else.

Also, I sit right down on the floor with the children. This makes me an equal participant in the daily events. A fellow teacher once commented that she hadn't seen me wear a dress all year.

It's easy to see why when you know how much I get up and down from the floor all day!

What's the Schedule?

Your coming-together time should include the introduction of the schedule for the day. At the beginning of the year, I show the children cards that have picture clues of the daily events. As the year moves on, the children add words to the pictures.

You can place these cards in a pocket chart in a linear fashion, as shown below.

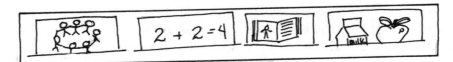

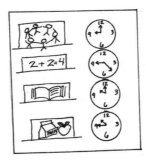

Or you can place them in the chart in vertical order.

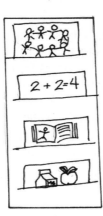

It's a good idea to place small clocks next to the picture cards so the children can see the time they will, say, go to gym class or have a snack.

As the year progresses, you can arrange your daily schedule in a linear fashion, with two lines. This helps teach the children return sweep.

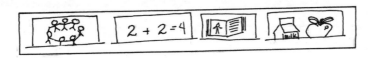

Let's Read Along

Tell the children that return sweep is what readers use if there are two or more lines of print on a page. It helps to have the children track the pictures or words in the daily schedule with a tracking device. This way you can see if the children are going from left to right and from word to word (or from picture to picture) and if they are doing the return sweep correctly. Some good tracking devices to use include the following:

- a glove stuffed with cotton batting and mounted on a dowel
- rubber fingers from Halloween costumes
- a back scratcher
- a feather duster
- a troll (The hair of the troll can "tickle" the words.)
- Bugles (These are funnel-shaped corn snacks that fit perfectly on little fingers. After the children track what they are reading, they can eat the Bugles!)
- a flashlight
- a dowel with a rubber eraser on the end
- Popsicle sticks
- straws (It's fun to blow on each word or picture!)
- a magic wand (Most anything with glitter will do.)
- a fly swatter (You can cut out the middle to frame the words.)
- wooden spoons
- mannequin hands
- fancy gloves
- puppets
- caps from markers (I put goggle eyes on them to make them look like little people.)

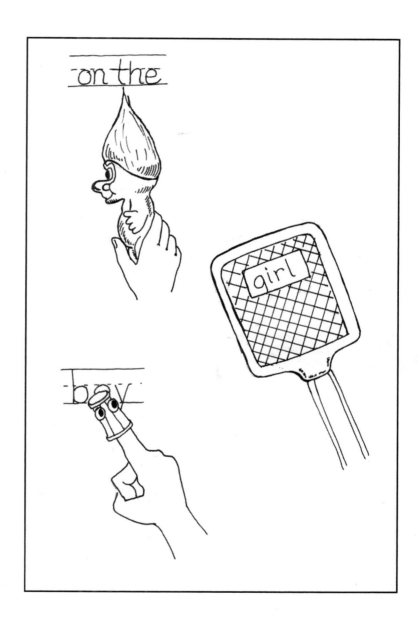

Your Opinion Counts

An alternative to the sign-in sheet is the daily graph, which contains a yes column and a no column. You can set this up so the children either write their names in one of the columns, as shown at left, or place magnets with their pictures mounted on them in one of the columns (see "Getting to Know You" on page 102).

At the beginning of the year, you can decide on the ideas to be polled or graphed. After the children catch on to the routine, you can have them generate the ideas.

Question & Answer

What should I do about the child who chooses never to participate during circle time?

I have several suggestions. The first is to wait the child out. There are many children who need a long time to warm up to a group situation and establish a comfort level with regard to sharing. If the child still is not participating after three weeks, you can ask him/her pointed questions, such as: "I see that you have a red shirt on today. What is your favorite color?" or "I thought I saw you smile when Morgan said she had a dog. Tell us about your favorite dog." Stay away from yes-or-no questions; ask questions that elicit an answer that requires more than a yes, no, nod, or shake of the head. And make sure the questions center on the child's world, like the examples I've given here.

It helps to have a special item that is passed from child to child in the circle. A person may speak only when he/she is holding that item. This is in the tradition of the Native American talking stick. You can use a stick, a magic wand, a smooth stone, or a microphone minus the cord. The children seem eager to share when they get the item.

Sometimes it is easier for shy children to share their thoughts through a puppet. Let the class mascot puppet sit on the shy child's lap and "talk" for the child. Or the child can first tell you something, and you then tell the class. Of course, you slowly wean the child off of you by encouraging him/her to take ownership of his/her spotlight time. This can be a gradual process, with you asking the child to clarify his/her thoughts as you repeat the general thrust of what he/she has said.

What's Up, Doc?

At the beginning of the year, you may feel more comfortable asking questions to give each child a chance to speak or to spur discussions. After a few weeks, you may discover that the children come up with their own topics and that your class meetings are becoming more child-directed. Below are some starter questions.

✎ If I were boss of this school, I would...

✎ After school, I...

✎ My favorite thing to wear is...

✎ If I had a million dollars, I would...

✎ I wish people would stop...

✎ I laugh when...

✎ My favorite food is...

✎ I hate to eat...

✎ I get scared when...

✎ When I get bigger, I will...

✎ The best thing about me is...

✎ I like school because...

✎ I am lucky because...

✎ I feel great when...

✎ If I were the teacher, I would...

My favorite food is...

Question & Answer

As the teacher, how much control should I take of our morning meetings?

I view the school year as follows: in the beginning, a meeting consists of about 90 percent teacher control and direction and 10 percent student participation. On the first days of the year, your goal as teacher during meetings is to model the appropriate behavior and climate. You should then gradually relinquish control of the meetings to the children as they seem to be able to handle the tasks, routines, and discussions. Your ultimate goal is to have the children take over so you become an active listener who redirects only when needed. By the end of the year, your meetings will become 10 percent teacher-directed and 90 percent student-directed.

Getting to Know You

On the first day of school, take a close-up photo of each child's face. Cut out the faces and mount each one on a small piece of magnetic tape. Paint a large coffee can (or cover it with contact paper) and label the outside "Cookie Jar." Put all the mounted photos in the can.

At circle time, pass the can to a child and have him/her pick a photo from it. Then you can play the word game "Who stole the cookies from the cookie jar?" The game proceeds as follows:

The entire class asks, "Who stole the cookies from the cookie jar?" The child who picked out a photo looks at it and shows it to the teacher, who calls out that child's name and then says, "_____ stole the cookies from the cookie jar."

The named child says, "Who, me?"

Entire class: "Yes, you!"

Named child: "Couldn't be!"

Entire class: "Then who?"

The named child then picks a new photo from the can, and the game begins again.

As each child's photo is selected, you can stick it to the outside of the can. This way, if you don't have time to get to everyone each day, you will have a visual record of who has been chosen already. Leave the can out all day so the children can take a look at the pictures mounted on the outside.

A variation of this game is to write the children's names on slips of paper and put them inside the can. This is a fun way to work on recognizing first names.

Question & Answer

Show and Tell seems to get out of hand. I find that sharing things brought from home takes up all the time we have for our circle activities. Any suggestions for managing it?

Having every child do Show and Tell every day can become a dreaded event. You need to use this time to validate the child who is "in the spotlight." Don't be afraid to set up a Show and Tell schedule where only four children a day bring in something to share. Set up a *Please Touch Museum* in your classroom where all Show and Tell items are put on a table where the children can view them during a free moment.

Other ideas:

- Send home a surprise box or bag with one child per day. That child places something from home in the bag, brings it back to class the next day, and gives the class clues about what the item is.

- Limit Show and Tell to one day a week.

- Have the children show their special item during snack time.

This way, they can go around to different groups of children and show their item at their own pace.

- Limit Show and Tell to the child who is the Star of the Week or the Special Person of the Week (see page 46). That child can bring in something for Show and Tell each day of his/her special week.

Conference Time Interruptions

Here are some ideas for what to do about children who interrupt you during your conference time (the time you spend with a small group or individual to teach needed skills).

What's an interruption?

Explain what an interruption is and why you cannot have children interrupting you during your conference time. State the obvious: Interruptions are distracting and prevent you from getting any teaching done.

Emergency 9-1-1!

This is a good time to explain the nature of a 9-1-1 emergency. Tell the children that if there is not a 9-1-1 emergency, they are not to interrupt you until you finish conferencing. I know a teacher who tells her class it needs to be fire, flood, or blood before they can interrupt her.

Have a sign-up sheet or board.

A child who needs help writes his/her name on a board with the understanding that as soon as you can get to that child, you will. When you get a free moment between conferences, erase that child's name from the board and see what he/she needs.

Make one child the liaison person.

Any child who needs you must go to the liaison person first and state his/her case. If the liaison person thinks it is important, he/she will interrupt you. (Most children do not want to tell another child about their situation, so most of the time this cuts down on minor disruptions.)

Create an interruption journal.

Have a notebook where children can write or draw their need. Tell them you will get to them during your next break from conferencing.
(I usually conference for about three to five minutes at a time, so I can get back to children in a timely fashion.)

Use a waiting chair.

Place the chair next to you, where a child who needs you can sit and wait until you have a minute to speak to him/her.

Have a hand signal.

Cut out an outline of a hand from red paper and one from green paper. Mount them on opposite sides of a Lucite frame. Turn the red hand toward the class when you are conferencing; turn the green hand toward the class when it's all right for children to interrupt you.

Drop names in a can.

Place a coffee can that you've painted a bright color in an easy-to-reach place in your room. If a child needs you, he/she writes his/her name on a piece of paper and drops it in the can. When you end your current conference, pick out the names from the can and go to those children.

Have each child draw a picture of himself/herself.

Label the pictures with the students' names and attach a magnetic strip to the back of each one. If a child needs you, he/she takes his/her picture and places it on a magnetic board.

Use a conferencing hat.

This is a hat that you wear to signal when no interruptions are allowed. Between conferences, take the hat off and let children ask for what they need.

Have an interruption light.

This follows the same premise as the conferencing hat. Turn it on when you conference, and off when the children may interrupt you.

Use the "Ask three, then me" rule.

Tell the children they should try to find help elsewhere by asking three classmates before interrupting you.

Of course, children will still interrupt you, and you will always listen, but you need to get at least a few minutes of uninterrupted time to conference with your students. The above ideas should help.

Grouping

One challenge we all face as kindergarten teachers is deciding when and how to group children. A multitude of research (Heibert 1983; Good and Marshall 1985; Allington 1983) says that the practice of tracking students (i.e., grouping according to ability) does more harm than good.

There are three types of grouping: whole-group, small-group, and individual. *Whole-group* instruction includes read-alouds, big-book reading, song and chart reading, group writing, literacy mini-lessons, projects, and other curricular activities. *Small-group* instruction includes guided reading groups, writing lessons, interest groups, literature/theme/genre focus groups, target skill groups, and instruction in other pointed curricular skills. *Individual* instruction includes assessment and one-on-one skill instruction in all curricular areas.

Whole-group instruction is done with the whole class, with an eye on each child's needs so that a wide range of abilities can be addressed. Questions can be posed to individual children on a level that is appropriate for their stage of development. It is important to remember that during whole-group instruction you are actually doing a lot of individual instruction based on what you know about each child. All children progress at individual rates, so your whole-group lessons need to address a variety of skill levels, maturity rates, and learning styles.

Kindergarten teachers are very attuned to the wide range of abilities that come through the classroom door on day one. We need to find out as much as we can about each child's abilities quickly so that we can begin to take each child to a new level. A lot of this pointed instruction can be done in a small-group setting or through individual conferencing. Do not make your small-group instruction into a lock-step format with rigid groupings. Rather, you should aim for differential grouping. This flexible grouping style changes as the needs of the children change. It leaves room for leaps and bounds of growth within a child as well as emotional speed bumps in a child's life that derail him/her from learning for a time.

Small-group instruction can be homogeneously grouped according to what you want to teach, the skill level of the children, or a particular need you notice in one group of children. You should not shy away from homogeneous grouping; you can change these groups according to your ongoing evaluation. This is a great way to give pointed instruction at a particular skill level to several children at a time. The catch is not to keep a high, middle, and low group. Instead, you recognize the need for reassessment and reform your groups accordingly. (Classroom arrangement for small-group instruction is discussed in Chapter 2, "Classroom Environment.")

Do not make your small-group instruction into a lock-step format with rigid groupings.

During the time that you conference with one child, what are all the other children in the room doing? This answer can vary, depending on the routines you've established. In my classroom, the children are eating a snack and having free-choice time. The free-choice play-center activities in my classroom include the following:

- sand table
- computer
- workbench
- painting
- writing
- reading
- listening lab
- blocks
- Play-Doh
- games
- puzzles
- housekeeping

If you do your small-group instruction in the middle of the classroom, other children will also learn while they sit on the periphery of that group. For example, while my students write in their journals, I sit with a small group of children and work on their journals with them. We work on writing skills, such as letters, sounds, punctuation, sentence formation, return sweep, and idea formation. During this time, I always notice that four or five children are "listening in" and thus learning from the same lesson.

Instructing individual children is by far the best way to address the skills they are lacking. Your one-to-one tutorial sessions can last from thirty seconds to several minutes. The key is pointed instruction, with one teacher and one child. This setup lets you really hone in on the task at hand and find out how a child processes information, how he/she produces the answers to your questions, and how much progress he/she has made since your last conference.

I individually conference with three to four children per day in a half-day kindergarten. For a full-day program, I conference with seven or eight children each day, during two separate conference times. These conferences last for about three to five minutes, depending on the needs of the child. The content is anything I see that the child needs to know; for example, how to print his/her name, recognition of the alphabet letters, how to pattern objects, one-to-one correspondence, or how to tie shoes.

I meet with the entire class as a group before snack so that they can choose their play centers. I explain that I need some time with the children I will be conferencing with for that day and that I cannot be interrupted during this time. (See pages 103–104 for a list of suggestions on how to handle interruptions.)

I make a large "centers" board out of a thirty-six- by forty-eight-inch piece of white cardboard. I keep clothespins, one with each child's name printed on it, in a can next to the centers board. I pick a name out of the can at random, that child selects a center for the day, and I clip the clothespin on his/her choice.

When the children get settled eating their snack, I call the first child and conference with him/her. Once our conferencing time is over, I usually let the child take a sticker or prize from the box of trinkets I keep at my conferencing table. Then I call the next child to conference.

Grouping children is nothing new. Teachers have been using this practice for many years, putting children into groups for writing, special interests, science study, reading, peers, literacy, catching up, learning centers, and the like. The key for successful grouping is to remember to continually reevaluate the children's progress and change your groups as necessary. Do what works best for you and the children.

Time Management Tips

Teachers are expected to reach unattainable
goals with inadequate tools.
The miracle is that at times they accomplish this task.

— Haim G. Ginott

To make your day's tasks more manageable, you need to look at yourself in a new light. Instead of working all day and into the evening, begin to think of yourself as the "queen (or king) of delegation." Continually ask yourself, "Can someone else do this job for me?" Not only will this reduce your workload, but you will successfully validate all those people who help you. Students, parents, and other volunteers or aides you enlist for help will feel a sense of worth and as if they have a finger on the pulse of your classroom. Of course, you won't give over the job of teaching, but you can relinquish lots of little jobs, thus easing your workload.

Once you decide what tasks you can give away or delegate, you can concentrate your energies on creating your class climate, establishing routines, and teaching your wonderful students. Below are lists of jobs you can delegate to others.

Let students do the following tasks:
- tie each other's shoes
- zip up coats
- open milk cartons
- help each other on the computer
- create things for bulletin boards

Let parents do the following tasks:
- cut out laminated items
- cut letters for bulletin boards
- create story boxes (see page 25)
- complete order forms from book clubs
- for more suggestions, see Chapter 5, "Parents as Partners"

Let aides do the following tasks:
- take the children to specials
- monitor the class while you are conferencing
- file paperwork

Let volunteers do the following tasks:
- run off paperwork
- type up notices, class lists, or schedules
- read with individual children

Concentrating all your energies on teaching requires you to trim down the extras you must get done each day. Here are some suggestions to help you.

Keep a tape recorder in your car

Your car is your office; use it as such. I get my best ideas while I am riding to and from work. Put a tape recorder by your bed and record your ideas whenever you wake up with a brilliant one!

Call yourself

Many teachers now have voice mail at their school. Call your own voice mail when you have a great idea or want to remember something. That way, when you get to school, you will have an instant reminder.

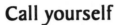

File

Try to file for at least three minutes every day. It saves so much time at the end of the week or during that mad rush right before parent-teacher conferences.

Keep a journal

Writing is a release for many people. Try keeping a journal of your thoughts and feelings. This can be a very reflective way to grow as a person and as a professional.

Organize

Put your work into six piles. Organize them as follows. (Or write your work tasks on a Things to Do List; see the reproducible on page 112.)

NOW!

Must do

Should do

Would like to do

Delegate

Throw away

Read

Subscribe to and read teacher magazines. They are loaded with great ideas, current research, new theories, and lots of teaching suggestions. A good source for titles and subject areas is the Educational Resources Information Center (ERIC). They have two helpful Internet addresses:

http://ericeece.org
(ERIC Clearinghouse on Elementary and Early Childhood Education)

http://www.ericsp.org
(ERIC Clearinghouse on Teaching and Teacher Education)

You can contact them by phone at the following numbers:

ERIC Clearinghouse on Elementary and Early Childhood Education (800) 583-4135

ERIC Clearinghouse on Teaching and Teacher Education
(800) 822-9229

Think "bulk"

Whenever you have a job to do, ask yourself if there is any way to do a little extra work to save for the next time. For example, if you're cutting out letters for a bulletin board, why not make ten of each letter and save the extras for later use? For quick letter-cutting, you, a volunteer, or an aide can use an Ellison die-cutting LetterMachine. [For more information, contact Ellison Educational Equipment, Inc., 25862 Commercentre Drive, Lake Forest, CA 92630-8804, (800) 253-2238; www.ellison.com.]

Use the dot method

Buy a package of small colored dot stickers. Code them; for example, red is for delegation, blue is for the office, green is for things to be done this week, and so on. Put a dot of the appropriate color at the top of each paper as you handle it.

Clear your head

There is so much thrown at us every day: new curriculum, more duties, more challenging students. Clear your head each morning before you begin your day and ask yourself, "What is the most important thing to be done today?" This will make you more focused and centered.

Get around

The best way to learn new things and get great ideas is to get out of the classroom every so often. Visit kindergartens in neighboring school districts, go to professional development workshops, and take classes. Yes, these things involve time and sometimes money, but they are worth every bit of energy you put into them. Ask your supervisor to route flyers for professional development your way. It does a person good to be with professional peers for a few days a year. It serves as a validation of our professional selves.

Use technology

Even if your only technology skill is knowing how to type, you should use a computer for your class newsletter and notices to go home. File and save everything. Get help from your school's computer teacher, a local college, friends who know about computers, and even the children in your classroom. I have kindergartners who know more about computers at age five than I am likely ever to know! This is the age of computer literacy; join in.

Write

You have great ideas; write them down and submit them to a teaching magazine. Getting published gives you a well-needed pump and boosts your professional credibility. Try submitting your writing to one or more of these publications:

Family Fun
244 Main St.
Northampton, MA 01060
www.familyfun.com
(413) 585-0444

Instructor
555 Broadway
New York, NY 10012
http://scholastic.com/Instructor
(212) 343-6100

Mailbox
The Education Center, Inc.
1607 Battleground Ave.
Greensboro, NC 27408
www.theeducationcenter.com
(800) 334-0298

The Reading Teacher
International Reading Association
800 Barksdale Rd.
P.O. Box 8139
Newark, DE 19714-8139
(302) 731-1600
www.reading.org

Talk

Talk with other teachers. We get such precious little time to connect with our professional peers. Make use of any time you can get. If you can't talk face-to-face, try these Web sites:

Instructor InterACTION
http://scholastic.com/Instructor

Let's Talk!
www.teachnet.org

Teacher Talk
www.mightymedia.com

Don't fret

Don't worry if you don't have time to put together fancy bulletin boards or centers. What really matters is your sense of caring, compassion, humor, novelty, and challenge, along with your love of your profession. Take comfort in the fact that all these qualities are within you.

Be healthy

Exercise, take your vitamins, and make sure you do something just for yourself as often as you can. You will be renewed by these self-rewards. Leave your job at school, and make sure you go home empty-handed at least one night per week.

Go easy

Remember that "effective" does not have to mean "perfect." The greatest teachers I know are filled with self-doubt. This quality is what continues to propel us toward greatness. Trust yourself and your instincts. You have today, you will do better than you did yesterday, and tomorrow you will do even better.

Question & Answer

Do you have any great ideas for the end of the school year?

Absolutely! Try some of these:

- Invite a kindergarten alumnus or alumna (a first-grader) into your classroom to talk about what first grade is like. Let the current kindergarten children ask him/her questions.

- Invite the first-grade teachers at your school to come in and be guest readers during the last few weeks of the school year. Meanwhile, you can go to the first-grade classrooms and read to your "old buddies" during this time.

- Invite parents to write about an experience that was special to them during their kindergarten year. Compile these in a booklet to send out over the summer to parents of incoming kindergarten students.

- Have a "favorites festival." Sing all of the children's favorite songs, read all the favorite big books, act out all the favorite stories, and recite all the favorite poems.

- Using all the photos you have taken of the children during the year, make a photo collage for each child. This is a job that you can delegate.

- Have each child bring in a pillowcase. Have them use fabric markers to sign each other's pillowcases.

- Make a memory quilt. Start by listing all the things the children remember from throughout the year. Give each child a six- by six-inch piece of white paper and have him/her select the memory he/she wants to illustrate. After you have approved the drawings, give each child a piece of muslin material and tape it at the corners to the tops of the children's desks. Each child then uses fabric markers to copy his/her drawings onto the muslin. Get a parent to sew them all together for you. This quilt will become your most precious possession.

- Take a photo of each child from the first day of school and one from the last days of the year. Mount them inside cards you make from pieces of white nine- by twelve-inch construction paper folded in half. With each card, include a package of seeds inside and print "See how you've grown!" on the front.

- Staple some pieces of paper together to make an autograph booklet for each child. Give him/her the opportunity to go around the room and collect signatures from each classmate.

- Get each child an inflatable beach ball and have each child in the class autograph it. It will be a great summer reminder for each child of all the friends he/she made in kindergarten.

- Have an end-of-the-year picnic with the children and their families. It is a great time to touch base with the whole family and thank them for a wonderful year together. Try to do this in the evening so working parents can attend.

- During the month of July I always mail my students the pictures I took of them throughout the year, along with a note of thanks and wishes for good luck in first grade.

Things to Do List

Plan for the week of_____

NOW!:

Must do:

Should do:

Would like to do:

Delegate:

Throw away:

Parents as Partners

Communicating with Parents

Communicating with parents is one of the most important things you do during the school year. Parents are your partners in the education of their children.

Children come from many different homes and types of families. As teachers, it is our job to find a way to communicate with each family in a way that will be understood and supported. No one way of communicating works for all families. The following list contains a multitude of ideas for working with parents. Choose the ones that work best for you.

Communication Tools

Newsletter

Writing a newsletter enables parents to keep a finger on the pulse of your classroom. Your newsletter should report the goings-on in your classroom, the subject matter you are teaching, upcoming events, weekly highlights, and any other information you deem important.

As mentioned in Chapter 4, I strongly recommend that you use a computer to generate your class newsletter. But it can be handwritten or typed if you feel strongly about creating it that way. The most important thing is that it should go home on a regular basis. I send my newsletter home weekly, on Fridays. If this is too much for you to take on, try sending it home biweekly. (See the sample newsletter on page 130.)

Home visits

Many teachers visit their students' homes either before the school year begins or during the first month of the school year. You will get a very illuminating view into a child's world through visiting his/her home. Make sure you call ahead and ask if it is OK for you to drop in. Set up a specific time for your visit, and be sure to show up on time. You need not stay long. Just introduce yourself and speak to the child and his/her parents for a few minutes. You may want to use this opportunity to give the parents any papers they need to fill out for school records.

School bus ride

If the children in your class are bused to and from school, it's a good idea to ride along with them one day during the first week or two. You will get to see where each child lives and connect each parent's face with his or her child. Even this short face-to-face encounter as you wave hello from the bus is a great parent contact. It lets parents know that you are committed to their children's safety and welfare when they ride to and from, as well as while they are in, school.

Question & Answer

What should I do about a parent who always brings his/her child to the classroom door in the morning and wants to have a conversation? I have so little time to spend talking to parents when the children should be my focus.

Make sure you state that by saying, "I must focus my attention on the children right now." Keep a copy of *Parent Journal* right by your door for parents to use if they wish.

Ask the parent to write down what he/she wanted to tell you, along with a phone number, and you will call him/her at a more convenient time to talk. Every time I have done this, the parent has replied, "Oh, it was nothing." The problem is solved, and the parent gets the message without anyone's feelings being hurt.

Touch base

Make a master list of all your students' names. Check off the names of students whose parents you touch base with during each month. Even a simple "hello" and a nice word about a child are great contacts. Look at who is left on your list at the end of the month and write a short note or make a phone call to these parents just to say something great about their child.

Comment page

When you make a class book for the children to take home for a night to look at with their families, include a parent comment page in the back. Simply add a blank page at the end of the book and write a note at the top like the one at left.

Children need an audience for their literacy experiences. Each child will be thrilled when you read his/her parent's comments to the class after they return the book from home.

Credibility

Pay attention to your credibility. Make sure parents know your credentials and your qualifications. Back-to-School Night is an evening, usually held within the first three weeks of the new school year, that's designed for the parents to meet the teacher, see the classroom, hear an overview of the curriculum/program, and become familiar with the routines of the classroom. It's also an excellent time for you to extol your virtues: Sing your own praises and state your professional accomplishments. Practice shameless self-promotion at times. Doctors' offices are filled with diplomas and degrees; hang up your accomplishments on your classroom wall, too. Get parents on your side before you need to ask for their assistance.

Networking

Identify the person who is the best networker in your group of parents. This parent will be the one who knows all the latest news and sends it around to everyone else. Make sure he/she knows the right information about your program and school. Don't leave room for rumors to start, because you will then have to waste time putting out fires of misinformation.

Face to face

As much as possible, have face-to-face meetings with parents. According to studies done by the School Board Association, 97 percent of people are influenced by face-to-face meetings. Only 3 percent are influenced by what they read.

Questions and answers

Each month, ask parents if they have any questions about your classroom and then put together a question-and-answer newsletter. You can be sure that if one parent has a question, there are five more who are afraid to ask it. All questions, no matter how trivial, are worth answering.

Lunch date

Invite parents into your classroom to have a lunch date with their child once a month. If you have a half-day program, ask parents to join their child for a snack.

Choose wisely

If you send home a class-made big book with a parent comment page or a class mascot with a journal, be wise when you select the first parent/family to receive it. Choose the parent who you think will model the appropriate response or activity the best. All the other parents will look at what the first parent wrote or did and model their responses in a similar manner.

One year I neglected to do this. I sent home a suitcase containing Heckedy Peg, our class mascot puppet, and a journal with a child to write in with his parents. The instructions said to return the suitcase to school the next day. But the next day it did not return. I asked the child to bring it back the following day, but the suitcase still failed to appear.

This continued for over a week. Finally, I called the child's mother and requested she send it back to class immediately. She said she would do so in two more days. I neglected to ask her why. I found out when the suitcase was returned at the end of the week. I took out the journal to read the excerpt the mother had written to all the children. Although the instructions requested that each parent use only one journal page, this mother had filled twenty-five pages of the journal with photos depicting her child with the class mascot at McDonald's, at the playground, in the car, visiting grandma, etc.!

Then, like a fool, I sent the journal back out in the suitcase with the next child. You can imagine what happened: every other parent thought that this was the only way to do it and followed suit. I learned that lesson the hard way. Now I choose the first parent wisely.

Smile

Take lots of pictures! At the beginning of the year, ask all parents if they would like to contribute a disposable camera to the class. Then let all interested parents know that some-time during the school year you will be sending a disposable camera to them to be developed. (If parents want to give something else to the class during the year, ask them for a prepaid film envelope.)

Have parents get double prints when they have film developed. Then you can use one set of the pictures to make a class big book to send home to one family per night. Save the other set for the end of the year. At that time, sort the pictures out; each child should receive approximately a roll's worth of film featuring him or her!

Some teachers I know make collages out of the photos to give to each child. I mail the pictures home over the summer with a letter telling each child what a joy he/she was to have in my class that year.

To relieve the hassle of sorting all those pictures at the end of the year, buy a large index card file box. File the pictures according to the students' last names. Then, at the end of the year, just pull each student's photos out as a group.

During the school year, when a roll of pictures is ready to be developed, I attach a short note to the camera and send it home to one of my parent volunteers. The note reads as follows.

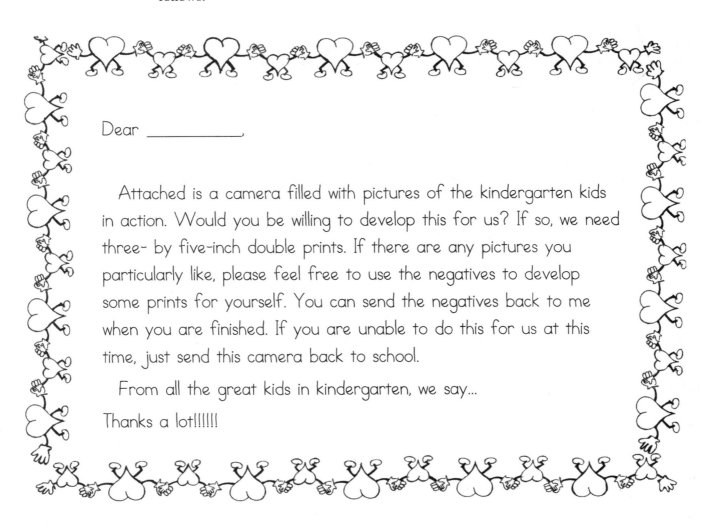

Dear _____,

Attached is a camera filled with pictures of the kindergarten kids in action. Would you be willing to develop this for us? If so, we need three- by five-inch double prints. If there are any pictures you particularly like, please feel free to use the negatives to develop some prints for yourself. You can send the negatives back to me when you are finished. If you are unable to do this for us at this time, just send this camera back to school.

From all the great kids in kindergarten, we say...

Thanks a lot!!!!!!

Conferences

I'm sure your school regularly schedules parent-teacher conferences in the fall and spring. Most conferences go well as you report to the parent the strengths and weaknesses of his/her child. But if you run into a problem and you want to record this information for future reference, use the form below. I use it to keep a record of what was discussed at a conference. I do not use it for every conference, but some teachers like to.

The form serves as a contract between the teacher and parent for the continued success of the child. On it I record the areas in which the child is strong, as well as the child's areas of weakness. Then I let the parent know what I am doing in school to help the child in his/her weak areas. At the conference, I ask the parent what he/she will do at home to help the child.

All this information is recorded on the form. The parent signs it; I then photocopy it and give one copy to the parent. Then we each have a copy to refer to. I have found this to be a great method for getting parents to really help a child at home rather than merely paying lip service to the idea.

Parent-Teacher Conference Form

Child's name: _Michael_

Conference date: _4/12_

Areas of strength:

- Letter identification, letter sounds, pre-reading skills

Areas of weakness:

- Following directions, listening to instructions, following and completing class routines

School help:

- Look at the teacher the first time his name is called
- Repeat directions directly to Michael; have him repeat back
- Take pictures of routines so the photos can be mounted on the wall and referred to as needed

Home help:

- Look at mom when name is called
- Repeat back directions
- Take pictures of home routine to mount and refer to as needed

Parent signature: _____

Sample of parent-teacher conference form

Parent-Teacher Conference Form

Child's name:_____
Conference date:_____

Areas of strength:

Areas of weakness:

School help:

Home help:

Parent signature: _____

Question & Answer

I am nervous about conducting parent–teacher conferences. Any helpful suggestions?

Yes. Here are some guidelines to follow.

1. Make sure the parent understands the reason for the conference. There is nothing worse for a parent than getting a note from a teacher requesting a conference but not stating why. The parent is then left to worry about what may or may not be wrong.

2. Schedule the conference for a time that's convenient for the parent. (Yes, this may have to be an evening time slot.)

3. Go to the parent if he/she cannot come to you. You can conduct a conference at a child's home or have a phone conference if there is no way of getting together.

4. Arrive on time (or early).

5. Practice pronouncing the parent's name(s) properly.

6. Provide a translator if necessary. Find one early in the school year so you are ready if and when you need to have a conference with non-English-speaking parents.

7. State your thoughts and ask the parent for feedback. After you say something, get the parent's thoughts about what you just said. Don't talk above a parent's head: Refrain from using educational language that only other teachers would understand, and keep your conversation jargon-free.

8. For clarity, restate your ideas at the close of the conference. Review what the parent has said and make an action plan.

9. Make sure you pay attention to details and comfort levels. Sit near the parent at the same eye level. Put a tablecloth on the table you use, and maybe even a plant or flowers. And tune in to the parent's body language right from the start. If the parent has pursed lips, arms crossed, and legs wrapped around each other, try to ease the parent's anger or anxiety before you begin your conference agenda.

10. Be yourself. You are the teacher; you are the authority. You know your business, and you know the educational plan that is best for the child. Speak with confidence and trust yourself.

More Communication Tools

Pack it up

Do you have some great books or articles that you would like your students' parents to read? Pack them up in a "parent backpack" that you make available to anyone who wants to sign it out. You can load it up with great books you've read or magazine articles that will help educate parents about their kindergarten child.

Teach

Don't forget that you can teach parents, too. Have after-school or evening workshops for parents at which you explain your curriculum, reading and writing with kindergartners, or ways for parents to help their children at home. Prior to your workshops, you can send out a letter asking for topics that parents are interested in learning about and use the responses to shape your workshops. Some teachers like to have monthly informal chat sessions where parents can all discuss elements of learning as well as their concerns and ideas.

Here are some topics to consider.

- how children learn to read
- how children learn to write
- how children learn to spell
- reading aloud to children
- helping children to learn at home

Connect to the past

Invite parents to come to class and tell a story about their lives. This oral storytelling has become a tradition in my class. Parents love it, and the kids do, too. You can learn a lot about a family by listening to their stories.

Thank-you notes

My mother was a stickler for thank-you notes, and I'm glad she was. I write a short thank-you for everything children bring me and to all parents who help out in any way. It's amazing what a simple thank-you can do!

ESL

For parents who do not speak English or who use it as a second language, you have to find a person who can help you communicate with them. I have advertised in the school newsletter and the town newspaper to find a volunteer to translate my weekly class newsletter over the phone to my ESL families. Because these parents miss so much due to the language barrier, you must take steps to make them feel wanted, welcome, and informed.

Classroom helpers

Inviting parents to help out in the classroom can be a blessing if you plan it well. I use one "contact parent"; this is a parent whom I call to request a month's worth of parent helpers and classroom-supply needs. He/she then calls all the parents of the students in the class to divide the duties. This saves me from having to spend an inordinate amount of time on the phone and ensures that each parent has an opportunity to help out if he/she chooses to. It also eliminates the elite "homeroom parent" syndrome, where one or two parents do everything for and with the class while the other parents feel left out of the loop.

You or your contact parent can find out what special skills parents have, times they are available, convenient times to call, etc., by using the form on the next page.

State your philosophy

If your school does not have a parent handbook that explains the school's philosophy of education, make one yourself and distribute it to parents. It's good to establish what your educational philosophy is and describe your program and curriculum. However, this should be an administrator's responsibility, so first ask your supervisor about it.

Instructions

You need to set some ground rules for successful parent participation in the classroom. Sending home a letter like the one on page 123 before they come to your class can save you lots of headaches. It clearly defines your expectations for the parents.

Parent's name: _____

Child's name: _____

Phone number: _____

Best time to call: _____

Days and times available to help in the classroom:

_____

Special skills:
___Baking
___Cooking
___Craft projects
___Sewing
___Computers
___Woodworking
___Outdoor/environmental activities
___Art
___Music
___Other:

I will help at home with:
___Cutting
___Project assembly
___Collating
___Art work
___Baking/cooking
___Donating needed supplies
___Sewing
___Typing

Here are other ways I can help: _____

_____

_____

_____

Reproducible

Dear _____,

Thank you for volunteering to come to our classroom and help us with our projects. Here are some guidelines to make your time with us go smoothly.

1. Before coming to the classroom, report to the office and get a visitor's name tag.

2. When you work with the children, use a soft, friendly voice.

3. Let the children do as much of the work as they can. You should assist only when you feel a child has done all he/she can.

4. Move from child to child in your assigned group, giving each child equal attention and praise.

5. Do not do for a child what he/she can do for him/herself, like writing his/her name or cleaning up his/her scissors, paper scraps, etc.

6. Focus on the children. Adult conversation should be saved for outside the classroom.

7. Do not touch, pick up, or handle any child.

8. Have fun. The children and I are thrilled that you can be here with us!

Thanks,

Reproducible _____

Show and tell

One of the best ways I have found to showcase my kindergarten program is to take slides of the children in action in my classroom and show them at Back-to-School Night. As the parents see their children in action—working on the computer, making patterns with blocks, interacting with books—it makes it easier to explain your program and gain parental support.

Question & Answer

What are some other ways in which I can gain community support?

Adopt a board-of-education member or a senior citizen (preferably one affiliated with the local seniors' group/club). Invite that person into your classroom if you have a play or puppet show. Ask that person to be a guest reader. Send him/her your weekly newsletter. Promote your class and your great activities. Then watch the word spread!

Display your students' artwork throughout your community. Buy a few inexpensive picture frames and ask the local dentist, doctor, bagel store owner, etc., if you may display a child's framed work of art each month. This is a great job for a parent to do. He/she could change the pictures in the frames each month. Don't forget to mention in your weekly newsletter that "Johnny's picture is proudly displayed at the Dunkin' Donuts this month."

Sing! If your class has learned songs during the school year, host a senior citizen or community sing.

There is nothing more precious than hearing kindergartners sing (and singing along with them). Everyone leaves with a glad feeling in his or her heart.

Discipline

Explain your discipline policy to the children and the parents early in the year. Keep it simple. Below is a suggested policy.

1. Keep your hands to yourself.
2. Walk, don't run, in the hallways.
3. Listen when someone is speaking.
4. Any other rule(s) you decide on.

Make sure the children and the parents know your discipline policy and the consequences that occur if the rules are not followed. One plan that works well for me is the discipline wheel. Each child has a clothespin with his/her name written on it. I explain to the children that I will keep the pins on this wheel. I tell them that if they choose to break the rules, then they choose to have their pin moved to the next section on the wheel. I emphasize that they are in charge of their actions, and it is their choice to break a rule. If a child breaks a rule, I ask him/her to move his/her pin to the next section. At the end of the day, all the pins go back to the beginning of the wheel.

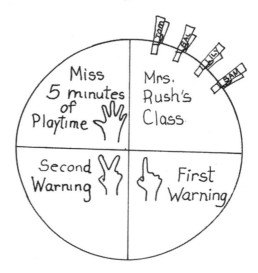

Little ones

Don't forget the little ones. Often mothers of kindergarten children cannot help out or come into the classroom because they are busy with younger children. Do something special for these parents (and your future students) by having a younger-sibling read-aloud time every two months. Invite the mothers to come in with their little ones for a twenty-minute read-aloud session. The brothers and sisters of these younger children will get a kick out of being the confident "older" child.

You're the best!

All parents want you to know is that their child is the shining star in their eyes. I send a short note home once every month to tell each parent that his/her child is terrific. If I have a particularly wonderful incident to report (e.g., a child helped a classmate when he/she lost something, or a child helped to clean up after a project), I tell that, too. I also develop our own kindergarten stationery every year by having each child draw his/her picture with a pencil on a three- by three-inch piece of paper. I then tape all these papers to the border of an eleven- by seventeen-inch piece of paper and run off multiple copies on the photocopier.

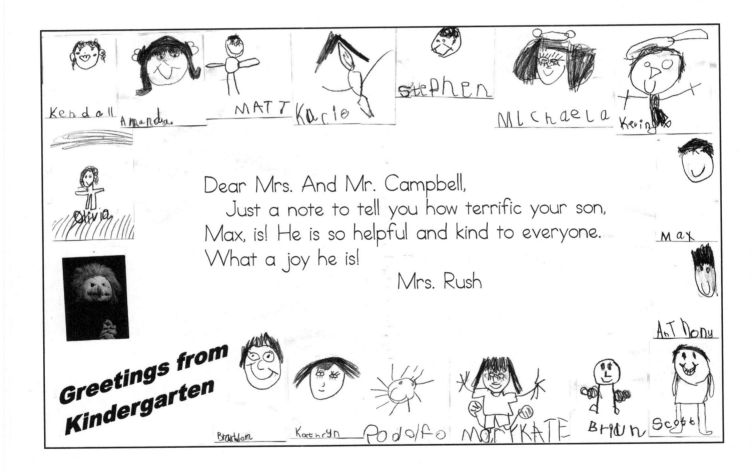

Dear Mrs. And Mr. Campbell,
    Just a note to tell you how terrific your son, Max, is! He is so helpful and kind to everyone. What a joy he is!

    Mrs. Rush

Greetings from Kindergarten

Ask for Help!

Volunteers

There are many times during the kindergarten day when it's great to have classroom volunteers to help with your program. Volunteers can be parents of your current class of children, and I love also to invite parents of children who were in my previous year's class to work as volunteers. They are familiar with your program and supportive of what you do, and they don't have a vested interest in just one child.

If you plan to use volunteers on a regular basis for activities that will be repeated daily or weekly, such as reading with individual children, you should have a volunteer-orientation workshop. This gives you a chance to stipulate exactly what they need to know before they interact with the children.

If you plan to use volunteers only once in a while, you should call them prior to their coming to the classroom and explain what their role and responsibilities will be. There is nothing worse than trying to explain the directions for a project to a volunteer when you have twenty kindergartners trying to get your attention.

Question & Answer

What if I cannot get parents to volunteer?

There are many other sources for potential volunteers. Among these are older students, grandparents, senior citizens, retired teachers, and college students majoring in education. Call your local junior or senior high school or community college and speak to the guidance counselor. Tell him/her that you are looking for volunteers to come to your classroom. I have the special-education students from the senior high school come to my class and read to my kindergartners once a week.

Try calling your town's senior citizens' organization. Many of these clubs are very active and have lots of members who love to work with children. I know of one school that has the kindergarten bus stop at the senior citizens' home and pick up volunteers on the way to school. At the end of the half-day session, the seniors ride the bus home with the kids! They love it.

I have also found that colleges are eager to get future educators into the classroom early on in their college careers. Students are willing to drive quite a distance to obtain some real classroom experience. Call a local college's education department and ask for volunteers.

Question & Answer

What should I do about the parent who wants to help out *all* the time?

Over the years I have had some very enthusiastic parents who wanted to help out or be in the classroom all the time. Instead of viewing this as a threat, I turn it around and consider it a blessing.

I first try to find out what the parent's motive is. Below are some that I have found in the past.

1. The parent wants to watch his/her child in action and compare the child to his/her peers. If this is the parent's sole objective, you will want to keep him/her out of your classroom.

2. The parent is studying to be a teacher and needs to observe and/or act as an aide in a primary classroom as a requirement for college courses. Often this parent can be a wealth of information on new trends and research. Such a parent is trying to gain a lot of information in a short amount of time and will be of valuable help to you.

3. The parent does not work outside of the home and wants to volunteer some of his/her time. These parents really do want to take on any and all projects you can give them. They are almost always gracious and sincere in their offer to help.

4. The parent wants to be noticed or recognized. Often such parents need you to validate them as "good parents." I have found that they often take up valuable teaching time by always trying to have a conversation with me so that I can see what great parents they are. This eats away at the precious little time I have with the children.

Once you find out a parent's private agenda, you can better gauge whether it would be worthwhile to invite that parent to spend a lot of time with you and the children.

If I have a parent who wants to help all the time, one of the very best ideas I have come up with over the years is to have this parent make "story boxes." These are story-retelling tools for the children to use during free-reading time.

Give the parent a copy of a best-loved storybook. Some of my favorites are *The Little Mouse, The Big Hungry Bear, The Red Ripe Strawberry*, and *Heckedy Peg*, by Don and Audrey Wood; *The Mitten*, by Jan Brett; and *The Very Hungry Caterpillar*, by Eric Carle. Fairy tales, such as *The Three Little Pigs* and *The Little Red Hen*, work great, too.

To create a story box, give the parent an empty box; a large shoebox or a photocopier-paper box works well. Tell the parent to read the book and then fill the box with anything he/she can find that will help retell the story. The parent can find things, buy things, or make things—whatever he/she comes up with. I also encourage the parent to involve his/her child in the creation of the box.

I have seen tremendous creativity come from the parents who make these boxes, which I keep for years! Over the years, my parents have made puppets, found slippers suitable for a main character, provided background props, and more. Whenever my class works on a learning unit, I pull out a "story box," and the children love to use the aids inside to do a retelling.

Aides

Working with an aide can be a blessing or a curse. If you really get along with that person, you will never want a year to go by without having an aide. On the other hand, if you and your aide don't see eye to eye, it can make for a very long year.

If you know in advance that you will be getting an aide, try to be involved in the hiring process for that person. Perhaps you can sit in on the interview or suggest someone who you know would be perfect for the job.

Working with an aide implies exactly that: You must *work* with that person, and he/she needs to know what you expect. Don't be bashful about stating your expectations right from the start and making yourself very clear. You will find that some aides are self-starters who will pitch in wherever they see a need, while others will hang back until they are told to do something. Make your needs and wants known. It is not fair to the aide if he/she always has to guess when to jump in and when to steer clear.

And, above all, say thank you! It works wonders when you let someone know that he/she is appreciated.

Kindergarten "Garden Patch"
Where Great Minds Grow
October 1, 1999

Reading: We have been working on the phrase "I love..." this week in group writing. We are sounding out these words to learn the individual letters and sounds. The children are drawing "picture clues" to help them read what they have written.

We read *The Old Lady Who Swallowed a Fly* this week. We worked on retelling this story and made a paper bag puppet to help us do this. I hope your child gave you a treat by telling you his/her version at home.

Math: We continued working on patterning and learning shapes this week. The children are making some two-color patterns, and some children are even using three colors. Heckedy Peg, our class mascot, is learning her shapes, too.

Science: We began a unit on seeds, plants, and pumpkins this week. We each planted a pumpkin seed and put it in our classroom Grow Lab. Take a look when you come in for Back-to-School Night.

Next week, we will begin a unit on insects. We will be setting up a Please Touch Museum in the classroom. Anything your child would like to add would be great. Remember to label everything your child brings in with his/her name!

On Tuesday, October 5, the Master Gardeners of Hunterdon County will be presenting an insect workshop for us.

Social Studies: We finished our big book about our tour around the school. We call it *School Is Cool.* It should be coming to your house soon.

Next week we will be learning about fire prevention and the use of 911. I am reviewing names, home addresses, and phone numbers with the children. You can help at home by making sure that your child knows these things.

On Wednesday, October 6, we will be treated to a visit from members of the Pattenburg Fire Company, who will teach us about fire drills.

Additional Information:

Lots of exciting things are coming up in October. Here's a list for you. You might want to mark your calendar.

Sample newsletter.

Tuesday, October 5, is Back-to-School Night, which begins at 7:00 p.m.

Thursday, October 14, is Kindergarten Date Night. This is an evening for you to have a "date" with your child. No siblings are invited; this is time exclusively for you and your kindergartner. It will take place in the school cafeteria from 6:30 to 7:30 p.m. This will be a relaxed evening of songs, stories, and fun, so please dress comfortably and casually. Bring a blanket to sit on and a book or two to read with your child.

The homeroom contact parents are:

Sue Murphy—a.m. class

Nancy Tarsi—p.m. class

They will be calling you to ask for any help you can offer, either in or out of the classroom. Feel free to help as much or as little as you like.

On October 20 and 22, we will be using paint for some projects. Please keep this in mind as you choose an outfit for your child to wear on those days.

On Wednesday, October 27, we will be presenting a play called *The Five Little Pumpkins* for parents (and grandparents, too). The a.m. class presentation will start at 11:00, and the p.m. class presentation will begin at 2:45. When you arrive at the school, please stop by the office and get a name tag. Then wait in the office area, and a class representative will come to bring you down to the classroom.

On Friday, October 29, we will have a Halloween party and parade. Please send a costume, in a bag, to school with your child on that day. Room parents will be there to help your child get dressed. If you want your child to have elaborate makeup, you can put that on at home. We will parade outside on the sidewalk in front of the school at 10:45 (for the a.m. class) and at 2:30 (for the p.m. class). You can wait on the sidewalk or down at the basketball courts to see us. We will come out the front door of the school, proceed down the sidewalk to the blacktop, and reenter the building through the back door.

We will begin our Pizza Hut Book-It program this month. Just read with your child for ten minutes ten times this month and initial the calendar. Then sign the calendar and send it in. I will issue a Pizza Hut gift certificate for a free personal pizza to each child who brings in a signed calendar.

Sample newsletter.

Chapter 6

Teaching with Themes
Picking a Topic and Presenting Your Themes

Kindergarten children are naturally egocentric and curious and enjoy charging head-on into investigative learning. Thus, using themes is the most natural way to teach them.

You can choose your themes based on either your curriculum or the students' interests. Each method has its merits: Themes based on curriculum are easy to plan ahead of time, while themes based on the children's interests are exciting, new, and refreshing. I have used both methods with great success.

Before you select some themes to cover, review your curriculum standards so you are sure of the specific areas you need to teach and assess. If you have a global idea of the skills and concepts you want your kindergartners to learn—for example, letter names and sounds—you can teach them under the umbrella of any theme you choose. Some standards, such as learning the five senses, can naturally be brought into numerous theme units. Each new theme you introduce can review curriculum concepts you have covered thus far as well as introduce, teach, and reinforce other concepts.

You should do all your theme teaching in an integrated manner rather than present every subject as a component or segregated part of the curriculum. For example, when you teach math, you also present elements of social studies. When you teach science, you also teach reading. A kindergarten child's life is naturally integrated, and our teaching should reflect this.

Getting Started with Themes

Review your curriculum

Brainstorm theme ideas by looking at your curriculum guide. Science and social studies, for instance, are good subject areas for ideas like holidays, ethnic traditions, the five senses, and plants and seeds.

Enjoy

If you are just starting out with themes, pick a topic that you enjoy. Use the reproducible graphic organizers on pages 138–139 for help with organizing and jump-starting your ideas.

Get help

Advertise your theme to parents and colleagues. You will be surprised by the wealth of knowledge, expertise, and experience some people have that you never knew about. (See the letter "Announcing a New Unit!" on page 142.)

Great books

Find some great books that will help give your theme a send-off. For example, a theme about insects could include such books as Eric Carle's *The Very Hungry Caterpillar*, *The Very Grouchy Ladybug*, and *The Very Quiet Cricket*.

Hands-on

Find items to go with your theme that the children can touch, manipulate, and experiment with. Create a Please Touch Museum, a special place for all items that can be held and played with. Put a green dot on each item to indicate that it is OK to touch it. Establish another space in your classroom called the Please Look Museum. Put a red dot on the items in this museum and establish a rule that all hands must be behind backs when anyone looks at the red-dot items.

Celebrate

Themes lend themselves very nicely to grand celebrations. Put on a play for parents, cook and eat a masterpiece based on the theme, make puppets to tell about what you learned, have another class attend a "What We Learned about _____" show, or publish a book of writings and/or drawings based on your theme. In other words, celebrate your knowledge.

What do you know?

Check to see what prior knowledge the children have about the theme you're covering. Write the two headings below on a large piece of chart paper.

What I Know About_____

What I Would Like to Know About_____

Have the children give you their ideas as you write them on the page. Use this as a springboard for more ideas for your theme.

Question & Answer

How do I let the children choose a theme? I don't understand this process.

I call it being an "educated follower." For instance, if I see some students bringing in lots of caterpillars and the other students zooming in for a closer look, this gives me an idea for a theme. I ask the children if they would like to learn more about different kinds of caterpillars and what caterpillars turn into. If the majority of them say yes, I have a child-initiated theme.

To get started, do the "What I Know About _____" activity outlined above. Use this to get the children to brainstorm ideas regarding what they already know about a particular subject and what they would like to know about it. The first few times you do this activity, you may want to prompt some answers to model the process.

Get a good look

Provide magnifying glasses, jeweler's loupes, or microscopes for children to take a closer look at items related to a theme.

Time

A good rule of thumb is to spend about two weeks on a theme. If you find that the theme keeps growing, extend it. Conversely, if the children show little interest in a theme, cut it short and begin a new one.

Theme library

Set aside a special shelf, book basket, or display case for books that relate specifically to your theme. Make sure you have a mix of fiction and nonfiction. Take advantage of this book collection to teach about the differences between fiction and nonfiction.

Dress the part

Be on the lookout for great clothes that let you wear your theme. How kindergartners love it when their teacher has a special shirt, sweater, or pair of earrings that matches the current theme! I have some great T-shirts that go with such themes as bears, insects, pigs, and butterflies.

Question & Answer

How do I make sure the children are learning?

Set your end goals at the beginning of the unit. Make a checklist of the skills you want the children to gain from the theme and then plan your teaching accordingly. For instance, if you want the children to come out of the theme unit knowing the three body parts of an insect, design the theme to teach that information. You can assess by asking the children to tell you the information they have learned, draw a picture depicting the information, or act out what they have learned. Once after I taught a theme unit about insects, one child crawled across the floor to show me he knew how an inchworm moved across a plant leaf!

Enough is enough

Don't worry if everything you present doesn't seem to exactly fit the theme. Just teach what you have to teach. A teacher I know once had her students do pudding painting; they had no idea they were also getting a lesson about the letter *P*, which was the theme of the week. (Of course, you should make your themes more global than a letter of the week.) But don't present anything so obscure that only *you* can make a connection between it and the theme.

Out loud

On a similar note, make sure you verbalize the reason why the children are doing a project. For example, when making a mobile, you can point out that you are doing so to show the life cycle of a caterpillar. Be sure you do all your thinking out loud.

To sum up, here are the major advantages of teaching with themes.

1. Theme teaching provides a more in-depth study of the subject matter.
2. Teaching with themes gives ownership of the learning to the children. You set the stage for optimum learning, and the children enhance it every step of the way with their curiosity.
3. Theme teaching acts as an umbrella under which all subjects can be integrated.
4. Teaching with themes lets you draw on everyone's talents.
5. Theme teaching is fun and motivating!

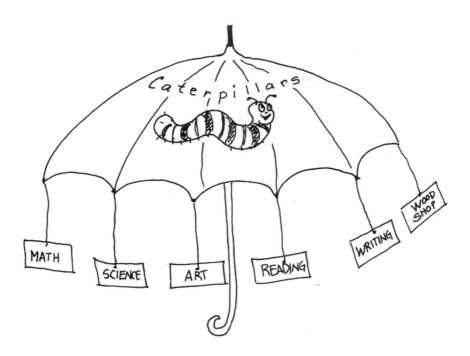

Teaching with Themes   135

Brainstorm

Brainstorm ideas on one of the Theme Brainstorming Sheets (see the reproducibles on pages 138 and 139). This is best done with a colleague or a teaching group. After you have lots of ideas collected, formulate a plan on the Theme Action Plan Sheet (see the reproducible on pages 140–141).

Theme Title: Insects

READING
Eric Carle books

WRITING
_____ are insects

ART
Make insect with three body parts from egg cartons

MATH
Graphing

SCIENCE
Identify three body parts: head, thorax, abdomen
View bugs with magnifying glasses

MOVEMENT
Move like a:
butterfly—light
bee—fast
ant—scurrying
praying mantis—slowly

SOCIAL STUDIES
Investigate ant colonies
Queens/workers' roles in the colony

MUSIC
Teach song "Head, Thorax, Abdomen"

MUSEUM ITEMS
Plastic bugs, magnifying glasses, bug boxes, glasses,

SUPPLIES
Egg cartons
Pipe cleaners
Goggle eyes
Bug boxes

OTHER IDEAS:
Call master gardeners
Pull up Web sites abo

Samples of Brainstorming Theme Sheets for a unit on insects (left) and one on farms (below)

Theme Brainstorming Sheet

Reading
Fact and fiction
Farm/farm animal books

Movement
Animal movements and sounds

Art
Make animal masks/headbands for "Farm Concert" book

Music
"Old Mac Vowel had a vowel: a-e-i-o-u"

Theme title
Farm

Social studies
Discuss and read about jobs on a farm

Math
Addition and subtraction using animals
Sorting and classifying
Graphing favorite animals

Science
Make butter from heavy cream
Incubate eggs

Drama
Act out "Farmer Joe's Hot Day"

Theme Action Plan Sheet

Theme title: *Native American Indians*   Date: *November*

Great books to use:
> *Knots on a Counting Rope, by Bill Martin Jr. and John Archambault*
> *The Popcorn Book, by Tomie de Paola*
> *Houses of Bark, by Bonnie Shemie*
> *Corn Is Maize, by Aliki*

Math concepts and related activities:
> *Review and reinforce plane shapes and geometric shapes.*
> *Use Native American picture/word symbols and housing shapes.*
> *Construct a longhouse and a teepee.*

Science concepts and related activities:
> *Examine bark that is used for longhouses.*
> *Examine corn with magnifying glasses.*
> *Plant corn, squash, and beans (the "three sisters").*

Social studies concepts and related activities:
> *Tell the story of the Legend of the Three Sisters.*
> *Make corn husk dolls.*
> *Make charts of Native American picture/word symbols.*

Projects:
> *Use picture/word symbols to make North ... pillowcases.*
> *Make "hide stories" with brown paper bags.*

Parent help needed:
> *Four parents to help assemble corn husk ...*
> *Four parents to help make vests.*
> *One parent to cut pillowcases.*
> *One parent to cut paper bags.*
> *Two parents to help plant seeds.*

Sample of Theme Action Plan Sheets for a unit on Native American Indians

Necessary supplies:
> *Popcorn, oil, and electric fry pan*
> *Corn husks*
> *Pillowcases*
> *Fabric markers*
> *Brown paper grocery bags*
> *Sticks and burlap for dolls*

Theme celebration ideas:
> *Make a Lenne Lenape Longhouse reading box out of a refrigerator box.*
> *Native American songs and chants with sign language (do a performance for the second-graders).*
> *Pop popcorn over an open fire (electric fry pan). Don't forget extension cord and an old sheet.*

Skills and concepts to be assessed:
> *Reading charts*
> *Learning songs*
> *Writing words*
> *Drawing stories*
> *Learning shapes, patterns, numbers*
> *Dramatizing Native American dance*
> *Science investigation of seeds, plants*

Method of assessment:
> *Assess shape identification via hand-held shapes and checklist.*
> *Check letter identification via charts, songs, and books.*
> *Assess ability to follow directions as demonstrated during multifaceted projects.*

Other information:
> *Check with librarian for other great books.*
> *Call Taylor's grandfather about his arrowhead collection.*
> *In the newsletter, ask parents if they have anything to contribute to the theme unit.*

Theme Title: _____

READING/
WRITING

ART

MATH

SCIENCE

MOVEMENT

SOCIAL
STUDIES

MUSIC

MUSEUM
ITEMS

SUPPLIES

OTHER IDEAS:

Theme Brainstorming Sheet

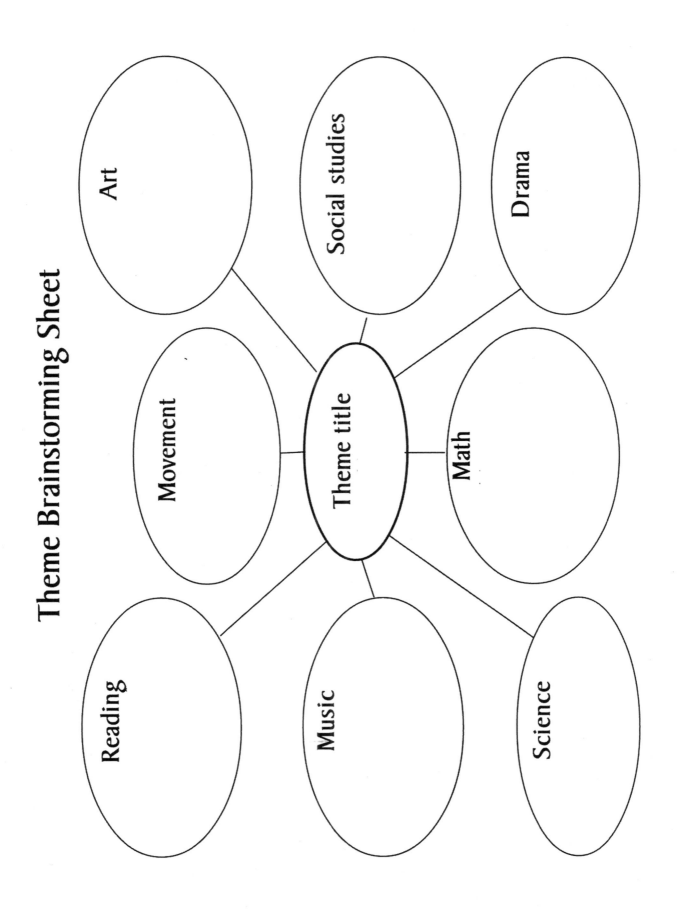

Art

Social studies

Drama

Movement

Theme title

Math

Reading

Music

Science

Theme Action Plan Sheet

Theme title: _____ **Date:** _____

Great books to use:

Math concepts and related activities:

Science concepts and related activities:

Social studies concepts and related activities:

Projects:

Parent help needed:

Necessary supplies:

Theme celebration ideas:

Skills and concepts to be assessed:

Method of assessment:

Other information:

Announcing a New Unit!

Dear Parents,

We are/will be studying all about_____ in kindergarten, and we welcome your help. Here are our needs:

GUEST SPEAKERS
If you know someone who could come into our classroom and be a resident expert on _____, give me his/her name and phone number. I will contact him/her about coming to speak to us.

SUPPLIES
We need the following supplies for projects we will be doing during class time:

MUSEUM ITEMS
If you or your child has anything at home that would add to our study of _____ , please send it in. Please indicate whether it can be touched and played with or not. Mark everything with your child's name.

BOOKS
If your child has any books at home that he/she would like to bring in for our theme library, send them in. Please mark all books with your child's name.

Thanks for all your help!

Reproducible

Ideas for Themes

Air
Airplanes
Alphabet
Animals
Ants
Apples
Babies
Bakery
Balloons
Beaches
Bears
Bees
Birds
Boats
Bread
Bubbles
Buildings
Bunnies
Butterflies
Cars/Trucks
Castles
Caterpillars
Cats/Kittens
Chickens
Circuses
Cities
Clouds
Coats/Jackets
Community
Corn
Costumes
Cowboys
Cows
Crabs
Cultures

Dinosaurs
Dirt
Dogs
Ducks
Eggs
Fall
Family
Farms
Feathers
Fire Safety
Fish
The Five Senses
Flags
Floating/Sinking
Flowers
Foreign Lands
Friends
Frogs
Fruit
Gardens
Giants
Grocery Store
Groundhogs
Hair
Hands
Hats
Hibernation
Holidays
Homes
Horses
Houses
Ice
Insects
Kites
Ladybugs

Lambs
Leaves
Light
Lions
Magnets
Mail
Maps
Mice
Migration
Milk
Mittens
Money
Monkeys
Museums
Native Americans
Neighborhoods
Nursery Rhymes
Nuts
Oceans
Octopuses
Opposites
Owls
Pancakes
Pigs
Pizza
Plants
Popcorn
Post Office
Potatoes
Presidents
Pumpkins
Rain
Rainbows
Reindeer

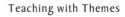

Rivers
Robots
Rocks
Roosters
Sand
Scarecrows
Shadows
Shamrocks
Shells
Shoes
Snow
Snowmen
Solar System
Spiders
Spring
Stars
Summer
Sun
Teeth
Toads
Traditions
Trains
Transportation
Trees
Turkeys
Turtles
Vegetables

Water
Whales
Wheels
Wild Animals
Wind
Winter
Wishes
The Woods
Worms
Zebras
Zoos

Substitute Teachers

Making Things Run Smoothly for Your Substitute Teacher

K indergarten teachers love their jobs so much they are rarely out of the class room. Every once in a while, however, you will have a professional workshop to attend, be sick, or have something else come up that makes it necessary to leave your class with a substitute teacher. Good organization is key: it will make for a worry-free day for you and a joyous day for the substitute and the children. Here are some ideas for making things run more smoothly for your substitute.

Helpful Hints

Names

The most important task for a substitute teacher to do is connect names with faces. A sub's calling the children by name will make the day run smoothly. You can make a seating chart with pictures of the children along with their names, but my students are rarely in their seats.

One technique I use that my subs have told me is invaluable to them is my "class ring." To make it, I use a set of photos of the children that I take on the first day of the school year. (I get double prints when the film is developed.) I cut out the face/head of each child and paste it on a three- by five-inch index card. I write the child's name alongside the picture. On the back of the card I write any information that a sub would need to know: medical conditions, allergies, after-school care, gets picked up from school by grandma, and so forth. I then punch a hole in the top right corner of each card and connect all the cards with a ring clip. Laminating or covering the cards with clear contact paper makes them more durable.

I hang the class ring right by my desk so it is easily retrievable. I also keep a lanyard-type string with the ring (a long shoelace works well) so the sub can wear it around his/her neck and keep his/her hands free to do activities. The ring also attaches easily to a belt loop. This enables the sub to carry the ring around all day and flip to the appropriate card to get a child's name or other information in a hurry whenever necessary. Also, the children love to show the sub their card and say, "That's me!"

Review

Unless you are going to be out of the class for an extended period of time, do not have the substitute teach brand-new information or begin units of study. It is an unfair burden to put on a teacher who is taking over for just a day. Try to make the information that the sub teaches review or reinforcement material.

Be clear

Make sure the sub understands the rules and routines of your classroom. Type them up and leave them pasted on the inside front cover of your plan book or sub-plan folder.

One year I neglected to specify in my plan book the signal the children used when they needed to go to the bathroom: a student just had to come up and tap me on the shoulder, I would nod OK, and he/she would go to the bathroom. This way, if I was conferencing or reading a book to the class, I did not have to stop to have a conversation with the child.

One day a student of mine came up and tapped the sub on the shoulder, and she asked him what he wanted. But he was a very nonverbal child, and he merely tapped her harder on the shoulder. She asked again what he wanted. The third time he hauled off and belted her in the shoulder! She shouted to the class, "What does he want?" They yelled back, "He has to go to the bathroom!" Needless to say, she felt I had a very aggressive class and did not want to substitute for me again. All this could have been avoided if I had remembered to put an explanation of the "system" in my plan book.

Prepare your students

If you know in advance that you are going to be out on a certain day, let your students know. If the substitute teacher is in the building on a day prior to your absence, bring him/her into your classroom and introduce him/her to the children. Explain to them that the day of your absence will be the same as usual but the teacher will be different. Reassure them that you will be back the following day.

Bag of tricks

I always leave a little basket filled with stickers, fancy erasers, funky pencils, and little toys for the substitute teacher. This way he/she can use them to reward good behavior and set the tone for expected conduct for the day. It has helped many subs survive a day with a large and active class.

I substitute-taught in a kindergarten class in Los Angeles one day with thirty-three children and no aide. If I had not had my "bag of tricks" with me, I wouldn't have survived past 10:00.

Follow up

Your school should have a Substitute-Teacher Reporting form. If it doesn't, use the reproducible form on page 148.

Go easy

A substitute teacher will not be able to accomplish all that you normally do in a day. Plan for uncomplicated tasks and easily understandable work, allowing plenty of time for the children to finish assignments. Add extra cut-and-paste activities or paper-coloring as time-fillers. The only thing worse than having too much to accomplish in a day is having too little. Make a coherent schedule for the day and highlight the "must do" things. Leave a note saying that it's OK if there isn't time for the other activities, which are extras to fill in time if necessary.

The buddy system

Whenever you have a substitute teacher, make sure a grade-level partner or other teacher comes in and greets him/her in the morning and asks if there are any last-minute questions. This teacher can make sure the sub is clear on routines and school rules and policy. If the sub has a problem during the day, he/she can call on this teacher for help. Make sure to return the favor when that teacher has a sub.

Great books

Keep a pile of best-loved books in a basket marked "Substitute Teacher Read-Alouds." These can be extra copies of books that you read and circulate among your students and that you know are favorites. If all else fails during the day, the sub can select a book or two from the basket to read, and the day will get back on track.

Ask the experts

I always tell my substitute teachers that, when in doubt, they should ask the children. They know the routines, rules, and requirements of the daily schedule and never let me forget anything. They will do the same for a sub. The situation in a kindergarten class is different from that of an upper-grade classroom, where students often try to pull the wool over a sub's eyes. Kindergartners are brutally honest and like routines to be followed.

Go for the best

If you know of a person who would make a good substitute teacher for your class, ask for him/her by name. Invite that person in to see your room and meet the children early in the year. Then ask for the same person to substitute for you every time you are out. I've been blessed with the same wonderful sub for three years now. She has become an extension of me, and the children don't miss a beat when she teaches in my class.

On the other hand, don't be afraid to request *not* to have a certain person substitute-teach in your classroom. I had a sub once who clearly did not enjoy children, and it was a horrible day for all concerned. Upon my return to school, I had to respond to at least six phone calls from parents who complained about the sub. You do not need that kind of aggravation upon your return to school.

Substitute Teacher Reporting Form

Teacher name_____

Date_____

Substitute teacher name_____

The following materials can be found in these places:

Substitute teaching plans_____

Class list_____

Daily schedule_____

Lunch/recess/bus–duty times_____

Medical or emergency information_____

Dismissal procedures_____

Fire drill information_____

Other information_____

If you have any questions or problems, please call _____.
He/she can be reached at _____.

Please use the back of this page to give a brief summary of the day. Feel free to include any concerns, questions, or things that need to be tended to upon my return.

Have a wonderful day!

Dealing with Struggling Learners

How to Help Struggling Learners Succeed

Every year you will have some children walking through the door of your classroom who are so deficient in skills and abilities that they struggle all year long. These children might be deficient for a variety of reasons, including being chronologically young, coming from an impoverished background, or having learning difficulties that are yet to be diagnosed. Below are some helpful ideas for working with these students.

Classroom-Tested Techniques

Find out what the struggling learner knows

Do baseline assessments early in the school year so you have a good understanding of what the child knows. Then work from there.

Frame the answer

When assessing a struggling learner, try to frame the response. For example, instead of asking, "What starts like *cat?*," ask, "Which name starts like *cat*...Catherine or Bobby?" Establish success; then move on to harder tasks.

Stretch it out

Struggling learners often have trouble saying quickly a word that is sounded out slowly. To help them, practice sounding out words while using a Slinky toy as a prop. Stretch out the Slinky while sounding out a word slowly: "cccccaaaaattttt." Then bring the Slinky back together as you say "cat" fast.

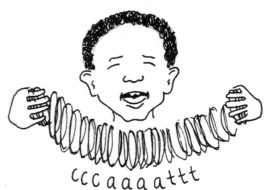

Rhyme time

Struggling learners have a very difficult time with rhyming words. Phonological awareness of words that rhyme is a skill that prereaders should have. Explain what rhyming words are and practice saying some rhyming words together, read rhyming stories, and play rhyming games. One such game can be played outside on the grass. Have all the children walk around in a circle while you say rhyming words. When the children hear the word in a series that does not rhyme with the others, they all fall down. For example, say, "cat, bat, rat, sat, pool."

Know the schedule

Some learners struggle if they don't know what comes next during the day's schedule. Hang a strip of Velcro across the top of your blackboard and attach pictures that describe a typical day's schedule. Let the children put the pictures for each day on a calendar as you discuss the day's events.

Quiet

Provide some quiet space or an alcove where children can get away from the throng of activity. A large cardboard appliance box turned on its side works great for this. Cover the inside with carpet squares to create a comfortable, quiet environment.

Remember that fluorescent lighting has adverse effects on some children. Let children wear sun visors or hats to cut down on overhead glare.

How do you feel?

Try some of these ideas to make your classroom a more comfortable place for all your students.

- Keep a fan on to move the air around.
- Use shades or blinds to block out hot sunlight.
- Remember that the warmest part of the room is often in the center.
- Allow children to wipe their face with a wet paper towel to cool off.
- Let children wear coats and hats during class if they are cold.
- Provide ear plugs or earphones to cut down on noise distractions.
- Offer pencils of many different sizes.
- Allow some children to walk around or stand up while listening to a lesson.

Remember the "six weeks" rule

You must allow six weeks for a change to have an effect on a child. Make sure you keep a journal of the changes you make and initiate only one change at a time.

Teach the hand alphabet

Teach your students the American Sign Language alphabet. Some children will come to understand and learn the regular alphabet through the tactile exposure to the hand alphabet.

Touch and go

Some children will touch, pinch, punch, and bother other children unless you give them something to do with their hands. Give them a Koosh ball to hold or a smooth marble to put in their pocket, or sew buttons on a large shirt and allow a child to wear the shirt and twist the buttons.

Up against the wall

Some children need to feel cocooned to be comfortable. Allow these children to sit with their backs against a wall. This will help them feel less agitated.

I've told you a thousand times

You will have to tell things to some children in your class many more times than you need to tell most students. Don't give up! Maybe on the 1,001st time they will get it!

Wait time

A typical response time for struggling learners can be as long as a minute or more for girls and up to three to four minutes for boys. This is a very long time to wait, but you must give these children the processing time they need.

Up front

Make sure the struggling learner sits close by you. This lets you check often to make sure he/she understands things clearly. It also lets you forewarn that child of upcoming transitions.

The bottom line

Ask yourself, "What is the most relevant information the struggling learner in my class needs to know today? What do I want this child to remember?"

Vary response modes

Raising a hand is not the only method a child can use to give an answer. Let your students cross and uncross their ankles to indicate agreement or disagreement with an answer or use a thumbs-up or thumbs-down to respond to yes-or-no questions. You can also use the following system, which gives a "way out" to children who often answer questions incorrectly: If they know the answer, they raise their hand and keep their fingers spread open. If they don't know the answer, they can raise their hand but keep their fist closed. This lets you know when these children want you to call on them and saves them from embarrassment when they do not know an answer.

What's on the front burner?

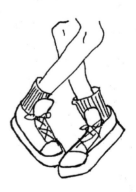

Some children come to school with monumental needs that must be met before any learning can take place. Has the child had breakfast? Does he/she feel safe? Find out what the child is in need of most. Can you try to accommodate it to help the child learn better?

Sing

Sing lots and lots while using charts. Matching spoken words to print is easier when it's done with songs than when it's done with spoken words.

Read

Marilyn Adams, author of *Beginning to Read: Thinking and Learning about Print* (see page 155), notes that the typical middle-class child enters our classroom with 1,000 to 1,700 hours of one-to-one picture-book experience. By contrast, the typical low-income child enters with an average of 25 such hours. Read to the children as much as time allows. Get aides, volunteers, or older students to read to the children one-on-one.

Check

Check, check, and recheck to make sure your struggling students understand concepts.

Laugh

Use humor in your teaching. Humor increases the retention of information by 15 percent to 18 percent.

Reteach

For some children, you must do daily reteaching of concepts before they can build on that knowledge. Take children from where they currently are on the learning curve and move them forward.

Get help

If you have serious concerns about a child's failure to grasp the concepts and learning in kindergarten, get help. Contact your school's Child Study Team or other professionals who can give you assistance in helping the child.

Retention

At the end of the year, you may have some children in your class you feel would benefit from spending another year in kindergarten. You cannot cause two years' worth of growth to occur in a child in one year. If a child is developmentally young, he/she may not be ready to go on to first grade. If you notice this, you should conference with the parents of this child every month. Work with the parents to make sure they know what you are doing with their child and how they can support the learning at home.

If you feel that retention is necessary, make sure that the parents support it. Retention will not work if they do not. If you have a situation where you have conferenced continually with the parents and worked with the child and the parents still want the child moved on to first grade, you should put an addendum on the child's report card or put it in his/her permanent folder. This will let the child's teacher for each subsequent grade know that it was against your best professional judgment to promote the child. (See the sample letter on page 154.)

Re: [student's name]

From: Mrs. Peggy Rush, Kindergarten Teacher 2000–2001

It is with reservation that I promote _____ on to first grade for the 2001–2002 school year. It is my professional recommendation that _____ be retained in kindergarten to gain the academic, social, and emotional skills needed to master the kindergarten program.

_____ has weaknesses in all of the language arts areas, including letter recognition, letter sounds, letter formation, sight-word recognition, and pre-reading skills. _____ has also had serious difficulty with the majority of the mathematical units this year. These include, but are not limited to, number recognition, number formation, patterning, pre-addition, pre-subtraction, and basic understanding of mathematical concepts. _____'s skills are at the level of a child entering a kindergarten program.

I find _____ to be a bright student with the potential for great success; however, it is my opinion that he/she entered the kindergarten program too soon. At this, the end of his/her first year in kindergarten, his/her abilities indicate a readiness to begin to develop the previously mentioned skills that he/she has yet to grasp. It is my professional opinion that, without these skills, for _____, first grade would be, at best, a constant struggle that could not only lead to academic deficiencies but have emotional and behavioral consequences as well.

Sample letter

Read More About It

Adams, Marilyn Jager. *Beginning to Read: Thinking and Learning about Print.* Cambridge, MA: MIT Press, 1990.

Areglado, N., and M. Dill. *Let's Write.* New York: Scholastic, Inc., 1997.

Armstrong, Thomas. *7 Kinds of Smart: Identifying and Developing Your Many Intelligences.* New York: Plume/Penguin Group, 1993.

Avery, Carol. *And with a Light Touch: Learning about Reading, Writing, and Teaching with First Graders.* Portsmouth, NH: Heinemann, 1993.

Baratta-Lorton, Mary. *Mathematics Their Way.* Reading, MA: Addison-Wesley, 1976.

Bredekamp, Sue, and Carol Copple, eds. *Developmentally Appropriate Practice in Early Childhood Programs,* rev. ed. Washington, DC: National Association for the Education of Young Children, 1996.

Clay, Marie M. *The Early Detection of Reading Difficulties.* Portsmouth, NH: Heinemann, 1995.

_____. *An Observation Survey of Early Literacy Achievement.* Portsmouth, NH: Heinemann, 1993.

_____. *Reading Recovery: A Guidebook for Teachers in Training.* Portsmouth, NH: Heinemann, 1993.

_____. *Writing Begins at Home: Preparing Children for Writing Before They Go to School.* Portsmouth, NH: Heinemann, 1988.

Cochrane, Orin, et al. *Reading, Writing, and Caring.* Katonah, NY: Richard C. Owen, 1984.

Cowley, Joy. *Whole Learning, Whole Child.* Bothell, WA: The Wright Group, 1994.

Crafton, Linda K. *Standards in Practice: Grades K–2.* Urbana, IL: National Council of Teachers of English, 1996.

Cunningham, Patricia M., and Dorothy P. Hall. *Making Words.* Torrance, CA: Good Apple, 1994.

Dorn, Linda J., Cathy French, and Tammy Jones. *Apprenticeship in Literacy.* York, ME: Stenhouse Publishers, 1998.

Ericson, Lita, and Moira Juliebo. *The Phonological Awareness Handbook for Kindergarten and Primary Teachers.* Newark, DE: International Reading Association, 1998.

Fisher, Bobbi. *Joyful Learning in Kindergarten.* Portsmouth, NH: Heinemann, 1998.

_____. *Thinking and Learning Together: Curriculum and Community in a Primary Classroom.* Portsmouth, NH: Heinemann, 1995.

Fountas, Irene C., and Gay Su Pinnell. *Guided Reading: Good First Teaching for All Children.* Portsmouth, NH: Heinemann, 1996.

Fry, Edward, Ph.D. *Phonics Patterns: Onset and Rime Word Lists.* Westminster, CA: Teacher Created Materials, Inc., 1995.

Gardner, Howard. *Multiple Intelligences: The Theory in Practice.* New York: Basic Books, 1993.

Goleman, Daniel. *Emotional Intelligence*. New York: Bantam Books, 1995.

Goodman, Kenneth S., Yetta M. Goodman, and Wendy J. Hood. *The Whole Language Evaluation Book*. Portsmouth, NH: Heinemann, 1988.

Goren, Ada H., ed. *The Mailbox Superbook: Kindergarten*. Greensboro, NC: The Education Center, Inc., 1998.

Hill, Mary W. *Home: Where Reading and Writing Begin*. Portsmouth, NH: Heinemann, 1989.

Holdaway, Don. *Foundations of Literacy*. Portsmouth, NH: Heinemann, 1979.

Ingraham, Phoebe Bell. *Creating & Managing Learning Centers: A Thematic Approach*. Peterborough, NH: Crystal Springs Books, 1997.

Jasmine, Grace. *Early Childhood Assessment*. Westminster, CA: Teacher Created Materials, Inc., 1997.

Jensen, Eric. *Introduction to Brain-Compatible Learning*. San Diego, CA: The Brain Store, Inc., 1998.

Kanter, Patsy. *Quick-and-Easy Learning Centers: Math*. New York: Scholastic, Inc., 1995.

Meisels, Samuel J., and Sally Atkins-Burnett. *Developmental Screening in Early Childhood: A Guide*, 4th ed. Washington, DC: National Association for the Education of Young Children, 1994.

Morrow, Lesley M., Dorothy S. Strickland, and Deborah Gee Woo. *Literacy Instruction in Half- and Whole-Day Kindergarten: Research to Practice*. Newark, DE: International Reading Association, 1998.

Moustafa, M. *Beyond Traditional Phonics*. Portsmouth, NH: Heinemann, 1997.

O'Connor, Anna T., and Sheila Callahan-Young. *Seven Windows to a Child's World: 100 Ideas for the Multiple Intelligences Classroom*. Arlington Heights, IL: SkyLight Professional Development, 1994.

Opitz, Michael F. *Learning Centers: Getting Them Started, Keeping Them Going*. New York: Scholastic, Inc., 1994.

Paley, Vivian Gussin. *You Can't Say You Can't Play*. Cambridge, MA: Harvard University Press, 1992.

SchifferDanoff, Valerie. *The Scholastic Integrated Language Arts Resource Book*. New York: Scholastic, Inc., 1995.

Shalaway, Linda. *Learning to Teach...Not Just for Beginners*. New York: Scholastic, Inc., 1998.

Smith, Frank. *Insult to Intelligence: The Bureaucratic Invasion of Our Classrooms*. Portsmouth, NH: Heinemann, 1988.

Snow, Catherine E., M. Susan Burns, and Peg Griffin, eds. *Preventing Reading Difficulties in Young Children*. Washington, DC: National Academy Press, 1998.

Strickland, Dorothy S. *Teaching Phonics Today: A Primer for Educators*. Newark, DE: International Reading Association, 1998.

Thomas, Rosalind. *How to Manage Your Kindergarten Classroom*. Westminster, CA: Teacher Created Materials, Inc., 1997.

Wagstaff, Janiel M. *Teaching Reading and Writing with Word Walls*. New York: Scholastic, Inc., 1999.

_____. *Phonics That Work!* New York: Scholastic, Inc., 1994.

Walmsley, Bonnie B., Anne-Marie Camp, and Sean A. Walmsley. *Teaching Kindergarten: A Developmentally Appropriate Approach.* Portsmouth, NH: Heinemann, 1993.

Walmsley, Bonnie B., and Sean A. Walmsley. *Kindergarten: Ready or Not?* Portsmouth, NH: Heinemann, 1996.

Weaver, Constance. *Reading Process and Practice: From Socio-Psycholinguistics to Whole Language*, 2d ed. Portsmouth, NH: Heinemann, 1994.

Wong, Harry K., and Rosemary T. Wong. *The First Days of School: How to Be an Effective Teacher*. Sunnyvale, CA: Harry K. Wong Publications, 1991.

Index